The
Get Clients Now! ™
Companion

———————— ❖ ————————

52 Power-Ups to Fuel Your Marketing Journey

C.J. Hayden

Wings for Business, LLC
San Francisco, CA

This book is designed to provide information in regard to the subject matter covered. It is sold with the understanding that the author and publisher are not engaged in rendering legal, accounting, or other professional service. If expert assistance is required, the services of a competent professional should be sought. The author and publisher shall have neither liability nor responsibility to any person or entity with respect to any loss or damage caused, or alleged to have been caused, directly or indirectly, by the information contained herein.

If you do not wish to be bound by the above, you may return this book to the publisher for a full refund.

CONTENTS

❖

i

PART III: Where Are You Headed? Goals, Priorities, and Focus

CONTENTS

INTRODUCTION

❖

Since 1992, I've been writing blog posts, articles, and columns to help self-employed professionals land more clients. For the first time, I've collected fifty-two of the most popular of these writings in one volume.

These pieces originally appeared in dozens of different ezines, blogs, magazines and newspapers. Many will be new to even regular readers of the *Get Clients Now!* blog and ezine. Each one has been updated to reflect current trends and conditions for professionals who market their own services.

I've organized the pieces in this volume into three different categories that match up with the first three chapters of the *Get Clients Now!* book: What Really Works?, Where Do You Start?, and Where Are You Headed? Here are some ways you might choose to make use of them:

1. As you are reading the *Get Clients Now!* book, dip into this volume for more ideas, encouragement, and clarification about the content of each of the first three chapters in *Get Clients Now!*

2. When working the 28-Day Program from the *Get Clients Now!* book, read one or two of these pieces each day to motivate and inspire your sales and marketing.

3. Any time you are feeling stuck or stymied by an area of marketing or sales, scan this book's table of contents to see which pieces might offer you some quick guidance.

4. Keep the ebook version of this volume (PDF or Kindle) on your mobile device, and read a piece whenever you have unexpected down time — on transit, on hold, or waiting in line.

5. Start off each week by reading one of the fifty-two pieces, and keep yourself fueled up to get clients for an entire year.

I hope you enjoy this new collection. If you'd like to receive pieces like this via email regularly, subscribe to the *Get Clients Now!* blog and/or ezine at www.getclientsnow.com.

May you find all the clients you need or want,

C.J. Hayden
San Francisco, CA

PART I

❖

WHAT REALLY WORKS?
EFFECTIVE STRATEGIES AND TACTICS

IF YOU WANT TO GET CLIENTS, YOU'LL HAVE TO TALK TO THEM

❖

"I've done everything I can think of to get clients," a desperate self-employed professional wrote to me. "I launched a website, I had a brochure designed, I've been sending out mailings, and I've placed all sorts of ads in print and on the web. But no one is hiring me. What am I doing wrong?"

This unhappy professional has made a common mistake. She has fallen into the trap of believing that spending money on marketing materials, mailings, and ads will somehow produce clients without the direct involvement of the business owner. And she truly believes that this is "everything" she can do.

Perhaps professionals who make this mistake are trying to follow the model of big business. They hide behind a company name, expensive marketing literature, and a website. They spend hundreds or thousands of dollars on ads, directory listings, and trade show booths. Far too many self-employed professionals don't even disclose their own name in their marketing, even when they are operating a one-person company!

But people don't buy professional services from an anonymous company whose name they don't even recognize; they buy them from either: 1) nationally recognized firms who have spent millions to gain name recognition, or 2) individual people they have learned to know, like, and trust. The more personal — or the more expensive — the service you offer is, the more likely this is to be true.

If you are a financial advisor, career counselor, or life coach, you are asking people to trust you with the most intimate areas of their lives. If you are a web designer, IT consultant, or corporate trainer, you are asking your clients to trust you enough to spend thousands of dollars with you. You won't earn their trust by placing an ad or sending a brochure.

Self-employed professionals and small professional services firms simply don't have the resources to build name recognition and trust by way of high-priced, anonymous approaches like advertising and mass mailings. In fact, the approaches that work best for most professionals to get clients are less expensive — and more personal.

Here are the five best ways for professionals to get clients:

> If you want people to become your clients, they need to get to know you, learn to like you, and believe they can trust you. And for that, they really do need to meet you.

1. Meeting prospects or referral sources in person, at events, or by appointment
2. Talking to prospects or referral sources on the phone
3. Sending personal emails and letters to prospects who already know them
4. Following up personally with prospects over time
5. Speaking to groups likely to contain prospects at meetings and conferences

And here are the five things self-employed professionals most often try that don't result in clients:

1. Placing ads on the web, in advertising directories, or in print publications
2. Distributing or posting brochures or flyers around their community

3. Sending generic emails, letters, or brochures to strangers
4. Sending their ezine or blog broadcast to people who haven't asked for it
5. Building a website or social media presence consisting of nothing but promotional copy

The main difference between these two lists is that the first group of approaches requires you to talk to people. The second list consists of anonymous activities that allow you to hide out and never meet the people you are in business to serve.

If you want people to become your clients, they need to get to know you, learn to like you, and believe they can trust you. And for that, they really do need to meet you.

It is understandable why so many business owners gravitate to the least effective marketing tactics — they are so much easier to accomplish! To buy an ad, all you have to do is put up the money. To send emails, all you need is a mailing list. It's much more challenging to go out and meet strangers, or to call people on the phone, or to speak in public.

But the reality is that this is what it takes to get clients. Even if you have the world's most compelling copy on your website, it's a rare client who finds their way to your site, reads it, and decides then and there to work with you. The same is true for an ad or a brochure. All these marketing tools are simply that — tools. Just like a pair of pliers, they need a person to hold them for them to work.

What clients want is to get a sense of who you are as a person. They want to see your face or hear your voice, to get to know you over time. If you don't have enough confidence in your business to speak to people in person about it, how will they ever have enough confidence in you to hire you?

What you'll discover if you begin to meet prospects in person, talk to them on the phone, and speak with them directly about how you can help them, is that it gets easier the more you do it. It will build your confidence in yourself — and the confidence your prospective clients have in you — at the same time.

If you're in the business of serving people, your best marketing tool can be your own voice. So, put it to work and start talking to them.

EVERYTHING YOU KNOW
ABOUT MARKETING IS RIGHT

❖

In over twenty-five years of advising individuals and companies on how to market their professional services, I have discovered something curious. One of the biggest mistakes people make in marketing is to not believe in what they already know. There are a number of areas where I've found this to apply, but here are three of the most important.

1. Advertising isn't effective. I don't mean the type of institutional advertising your parent company does when you own a franchise. Nor do I mean the product advertising that blankets the media and clutters your mailbox and computer screen. What I mean is you as a self-employed professional or small services firm. Advertising simply doesn't make much sense for *you*.

For the solo professional, there's no economy of scale. You don't have the earning potential to pay for the amount of advertising that would make a difference. As a small services firm, you can afford it if you're big enough, but it's rarely the best use of your financial resources. Not when you have those talented human resources on hand to carry out other more effective strategies.

2. Talking to prospective clients works. How do you talk to them? Attend meetings where they congregate, place follow-up phone calls, schedule lunch and coffee dates, speak in public. Using the same approaches with those who can refer clients to you is just as valuable.

Why do these tactics work when advertising doesn't? Because they build the critical know-like-and-trust factor that makes people choose a professional to provide an essential service. Services are intangible; you can't see, touch, or taste them until they are demonstrated. When you purchase a service, you must rely on your judgment about the person delivering it.

If a potential client gets to know you, learns to like you, and believes that he or she can trust you, you probably have a sale. Advertising not only can't create this for you, it can actually interfere with it. Would you choose a life insurance agent who you saw advertising on late night TV?

> Consistency builds the know-like-and-trust factor; it establishes you as a presence in the minds of your intended clients.

3. You must be consistent and persistent. Do the same things over and over, whether or not you feel like it. Make a certain number of calls, go to so many meetings, keep following up with likely prospects, week in, week out, month after month.

Consistency builds the know-like-and-trust factor; it establishes you as a presence in the minds of your intended clients. Persistence keeps you going when results aren't immediate; it's what eventually closes the sale.

Am I right? Did you already know these three essential principles? But if we reviewed what you've actually done about marketing in the past year, I'll bet it would look like you had forgotten at least one of them.

Perhaps you were tempted by an advertising special, or were lured into thinking advertising would be an "easier" way to get clients. Or you spent all your marketing time developing a website and setting up social media profiles, instead of talking with people already in your network.

Maybe you kept finding more important things to do than get out of your office and meet people. Or phone phobia took over and weeks went by before you placed some important calls.

It could be you thought you'd try your hand at generating some publicity, and dropped the ball on following through with existing leads while your attention was diverted elsewhere. Maybe you got busy with paying work and stopped marketing. Either way, your consistency suffered, or you ceased being persistent.

Or maybe, like so many others I know, you were sidetracked by the quest for the magic formula, the secret key, the silver bullet that will take all the effort out of marketing your professional services and send you an endless stream of clients forever.

Okay, I won't keep you in suspense any longer — here is the magic formula you've been seeking. Spend your time talking to prospective clients, don't rely on advertising, and be consistent and persistent in your marketing.

But you already knew that.

MAKE YOUR MARKETING
WORK SMARTER, NOT HARDER

❖

I've been asking successful self-employed professionals lately what it was they did that finally launched their success. What activity helped them the most to stop struggling to market themselves and start finding clients with more ease?

The diversity of their answers has been intriguing, but I've been struck by what they haven't said as well as what they have. So far, not a single person has told me they ultimately got more results from their marketing by working harder.

This may seem to be at odds with what we learn about marketing from books, classes, and consultants. Given the volume and variety of ideas these experts share with us, aren't they suggesting we need to do "more?" Or is it possible that the message to work harder is just our own interpretation? Perhaps what the experts are really advising is something different.

There is a certain threshold of marketing activity every professional needs to cross. You can't sit in your office communicating with no one and expect clients to arrive at your door. Nor can you accomplish results with your marketing if you don't make time for it in your calendar. But once you are regularly taking action about marketing, the secret to success appears to be working smarter, not harder.

How do you tell the difference between working harder at marketing and working smarter? Here are some comparisons:

Harder: Place more cold calls to new prospects.
Smarter: Follow up regularly with warm calls to people with whom you already have a connection.

Harder: Launch a direct mail campaign, sending sales letters to a prospect list you purchased or compiled from public sources.

Smarter: Send personal email or letters to people whose problems and goals you have some knowledge of.

Harder: Attend more networking events.

Smarter: Attend only those events frequented by people in your target market or by likely referral partners.

> Take a lesson from the successful professionals who assert that simply working harder isn't the whole answer.

Harder: Ask everyone you come in contact with to refer business to you.

Smarter: Spend time building relationships with key people who are likely to be in contact with your ideal clients.

Harder: Build the biggest network you can on multiple social media platforms, and interact on all of them daily.

Smarter: Choose one social media platform your clients use for relevant interactions, build a network appropriate to your business, and spend a limited amount of time there regularly.

Harder: Book every speaking engagement you can get.

Smarter: Accept speaking engagements only when the topic draws on the core of your expertise and the audience is the right profile for your services.

Harder: Write a new, original article for every publication you run across that might publish your work.

Smarter: Seek out publications that appeal to your target audience and submit previously-published (or slightly revised) pieces to multiple venues.

What you may notice about these examples is that the "work harder" path in some ways can seem easier than the "work smarter" one. For example, you don't have to think very much to make more cold calls. You can simply sit down with a list you got from anywhere, smile, and dial. But to follow up regularly with people you already know, you need to have a system in place to keep track of when you last conversed and what you talked about.

Similarly, to attend more networking events, without too much thought you can probably see what's being advertised somewhere or arrives in your mailbox, register, and show up. But to attend only events relevant to your target market, you need to craft a clear definition of who that market is and do some homework to seek out events where those people gather.

Is there any point, though, in doing more just because it's easier, if in fact what you are doing is considerably less likely to produce results?

Take a lesson from the successful professionals who assert that simply working harder isn't the whole answer. However you are currently marketing your business — making calls, attending events, etc. — ask yourself how you can improve those strategies by applying more focus and direction instead of just more time and effort. To make your marketing more successful, take off your running shoes and put your thinking cap on.

IN MARKETING,
THE INTERNET IS NOT THE UNIVERSE
❖

"I have a great website and publish a regular blog," my client complained, "but I'm not getting any clients from it. The only new client I got this month was a referral from a friend. What am I doing wrong?"

It's a common complaint of self-employed professionals that they spend a great deal of time and money on Internet marketing and social media with minimal results. You build an attractive website, launch an ezine or blog, set up a couple of social media profiles, and maybe try a Google AdWords campaign. But for all that effort, not much seems to come of it. What's going on?

There's so much hype about online marketing that it's easy to lose sight of some of the basic marketing principles for professional services. To begin with, much of the marketing online is nothing more than advertising, and advertising is, overall, the least effective marketing strategy a self-employed professional can use.

A website that says simply, "hire me," with no educational or interactive content included, is just a large, expensive ad. Unless you put even more effort into attracting people to visit, this ad doesn't even have much circulation.

Other forms of online marketing that fall into the category of advertising are any post or broadcast that contains little helpful content for the reader (these could be ezines, blog posts, social media posts, or broadcast emails), online directory listings, and of course, banner or text ads that you pay for.

If advertising is at the bottom of the list as far as effectiveness, what's at the top? For self-employed professionals, the three most effective marketing strategies, in this order, are:

1. Direct personal contact with prospects
2. Networking and referral building
3. Public speaking

Of course, all three of these strategies can be employed online. You can send personal emails to prospects and referral sources, make networking contacts via email or social media, and speak via webinars and teleclasses advertised online. But why limit those strategies to the Internet?

> The answer lies in recognizing that the Internet is not a marketing strategy; it's a marketing medium…

The reality is that for most self-employed professionals, direct contact with prospects is more effective in person and on the phone than it is by email. Networking and referral building, even though it may begin with an online contact, gets its power from the personal relationships you build by interacting with people one-on-one. And virtual public speaking is great for reaching people outside your area, but when most of your clients are local, speaking to them in person has much more impact.

Notice that my client who complained online marketing wasn't working stepped right over what *was* working. A friend had referred him business. More questions uncovered that he had lunch with that friend shortly before the referral. So, if that produced a client, and his website hasn't, why not schedule more lunches instead of doing more online?

The online world can be a useful setting for marketing, but it's not the whole universe. As recently as fifteen years ago, millions of professionals were successfully marketing their services without using the web at all. They called people on the phone, sent letters, met with prospects in person, had coffee with referral sources, and spoke to live audiences. If you think about it, it's obvious that none of those techniques have *stopped* working just because the Internet now exists.

So, the one remaining question is whether online marketing is somehow more effective than traditional forms of marketing. The answer lies in recognizing that the Internet is not a marketing strategy; it's a marketing medium, like the telephone, for example, or postal mail. Its power depends on how you use it, not on whether you use it or not.

The same basic principles of professional services marketing still apply, regardless of what medium you use. The most effective strategies are those that include personal contact and build trust and credibility, like the three I mentioned above. If you can do those things better or more efficiently online than on the phone or in person, by all means, use the web for marketing. But before choosing to rely on the Internet as your sole source of clients, think twice.

Marketing your business exclusively online often serves as a handy excuse for not talking to people. It's all too easy to hide out behind a website, email, and social media, and never experience rejection or step outside your comfort zone.

Marketing done the old-fashioned way — calling prospects on the phone, attending networking events, asking people to lunch — may be much more confronting. Those live, personal conversations, though, may be just what your marketing needs to take off.

If you've been feeling stuck about getting clients, try getting off the web for a while. Instead, get on the phone, and get out of your office. There's a whole world out there of people eager to talk to a live person. You may just find that marketing in person turns out to be not only more effective, but more enjoyable, than marketing online.

DON'T WAIT FOR WORD OF MOUTH

❖

Self-employed professionals who have been operating for a while always say they get most of their clients by word of mouth. But if you're relatively new in business, no one is talking about you yet. How can you start building word of mouth right away instead of just waiting for it to happen?

The fastest and most effective way to do this is by actively working to generate referrals. A referral acts as an endorsement for your business. A prospective client who is referred to you by someone they trust is much more likely to hire you than a client you attract through advertising or promotion. Referred clients are also less likely to question your credentials or rates, so you can close sales more quickly.

Referrals come from a wide variety of sources, including satisfied customers, your friends and family, colleagues and competitors, and business owners who share the same market niche as you. Here are a few ways you can work with each group to increase the number of referrals they give you.

1. Satisfied customers are often a good source of referrals. When your list of past clients is short, you'll need to put more effort into keeping in touch with each one. After completing a client project, give your clients a call a few weeks afterward to ask how well what you did is working out for them. Invite former clients to coffee or lunch, or to business or social events you're planning to attend. Consider hosting an annual open house or free workshop to thank clients for doing business with you.

Don't contact past clients just to ask them to refer you more business. Instead, contact them regularly with information, resources, or invitations that they will find valuable. These contacts can take the form of phone calls, emails, a regular newsletter or ezine, blog posts sent by email, or a postcard series. To generate the maximum number of referrals, you should be in touch once per month, but if not, make sure it's at least three to four times per year.

2. Personal friends and family can send plenty of business your way if they know enough about what you do. Don't be afraid to include them on your mailing list and invite them to your business events. They already know and love you, and will be happy to help your business grow — just ask them.

> Spend some time brainstorming about the categories of businesses that serve your marketplace, and begin to seek these people out.

Since these people may not understand your business well, tell them exactly what kind of clients you are looking for, and when a referral might be appropriate. For example, a chiropractor might suggest that family members refer people when they hear them complain of back pain or an injury from an accident. A technical writer could tell friends that a good referral for her would be someone in the financial services field who mentions the upcoming release of a new product.

3. Colleagues and competitors will refer you clients under many circumstances. Perhaps you have a specialty or expertise that they don't, or they have more business than they can handle at times. Get to know other people in your field through your professional association or a local business network. Ask colleagues you already know to introduce you to others. Or just look them up and make contact.

Propose a referral partnership, where the two of you will be on the lookout for clients you can potentially refer to each other. Not everyone will be open to this idea, but you'll find that some people will be enthusiastic about it. Keep in mind that the only real difference between a colleague and a competitor may be your attitude about them.

4. Business owners who share your market niche are in contact with your prospective clients all the time. If you can form referral partnerships with a variety of businesses in different fields but the same market, you will create a far-reaching referral network. For example, a marketing consultant might get to know graphic designers, business planning consultants, bankers, and accountants, all of whom have regular contact with businesses looking to grow.

Spend some time brainstorming about the categories of businesses that serve your marketplace, and begin to seek these people out. Ask the people you already know who they know. You could gain introductions to many accountants, for example, just by asking your friends and colleagues who does their taxes. If the referral relationship you are offering is reciprocal, savvy entrepreneurs will welcome your approach, even if they don't yet know you.

Finally, to generate more referrals from every group, remember to thank the people who refer business to you, even when a referral doesn't turn into a client. The more thanks you give, the more referrals you will ultimately get.

CAN'T I HIRE SOMEONE TO MARKET ME?

❖

"I'm really good at what I do, but marketing isn't my strong point. If someone else could develop the leads and book appointments for me, I'm sure I could land more clients once I got the chance to talk to them. Can't I just hire someone to do my marketing for me?"

It sounds appealing, doesn't it? No more networking, soliciting referrals, sending emails and letters, speaking in public, writing blog posts and articles, standing around at trade shows, and finally — no more cold calls.

Yes, you could hire someone: a contract marketing representative, commissioned salesperson, or telemarketer. A marketing rep will search out leads, make the initial contact, and sometimes even make a presentation to the client alone or along with you. Contract reps often work on retainer, plus a bonus when they close a deal. Reps can't guarantee that they will land you clients, and you pay the retainer no matter what.

A salesperson will make contacts for you and present your business to prospects. Some salespeople will research their own leads; others expect you to tell them who to contact. If the potential return is high enough, salespeople will work on straight commission — you pay them only when a sale is made.

Telemarketers will make telephone contact with the prospects you target, and try to set up appointments for you. You need to provide the telemarketer with a list, which you can purchase from a list broker or compile from directories or membership and subscription lists. Telemarketers expect to be paid for their time, whether or not their calls are successful. You typically give them an added incentive by offering a bonus for each appointment they make.

But here's the reality. Unless you are operating a firm with several principals available to provide service to clients, hiring someone to market for you will probably be a waste of money. For professionals, consultants, or coaches running a one- or two-person shop, your earning power is limited by the number of clients you can individually serve. Unless your rates are already quite high, it will be difficult for you to bring in enough money to pay for talented marketing help and still make a profit.

For example, if you charge $100 per hour, and bill 22 hours per week (a typical average for consultants), your maximum earnings are $2200 weekly. If you pay a salesperson 15% commission on that, he or she gets $330 per week. What quality of salesperson will you get for that amount of money? How much time will he or she be willing to spend on your account? Can you see that you would have to pay much more to keep a skilled salesperson working for you?

> ...a business without an effective marketing arm is not yet a viable business.

If this example makes you think you'd rather hire a telemarketer by the hour, consider this. Could a telemarketer give the kind of answers prospective clients typically need when you get them on the phone? Clients resent being called on by an uninformed person. Unless you are prepared to spend many hours working with a telemarketer to bring him or her up to speed (and pay for the time), this approach is rarely effective, and may backfire with potential clients.

The most you can realistically expect from a telemarketer is to make calls with the purpose of identifying the right person within an organization, verifying or obtaining contact information, or delivering a message or invitation. A productive use of telemarketers can be to inform prospects to watch for a mailing from you or remind them of an upcoming seminar. But you still have to provide them with the list of people to call.

Making cold calls to a list of strangers is one of the least effective ways for a professional to market. Even with a relatively low-paid telemarketer placing the calls instead of you, the ratio of appointments to calls is likely to be so low that your investment won't pay off. For an approach like this to be successful, your telemarketer needs a prospect list of people already familiar with your work. Building a list like that, of course, requires marketing, which someone else will still have to do.

Unfortunately, a business without an effective marketing arm is not yet a viable business. Successful professional practice firms always have at least one principal owner who brings in the clients. When you're the only owner; learning to market yourself is an absolute necessity.

If you find it too difficult to learn marketing skills yourself (or simply don't want to), consider partnering with a colleague who was born with the marketing gene. Or, subcontract your services to a larger firm instead of trying to land your own clients. You will have to give up a percentage of income that way, just as if you were paying someone to market you. But, you'll avoid the mistake of paying for marketing help that doesn't pay for itself.

MAKE YOUR WEBSITE WORK MORE
SO YOU CAN WORK LESS

❖

Do you know how your website fits into the overall marketing strategy for your business? Do you have a strategy for your website as a marketing tool? If you're like many self-employed professionals I speak with, you probably don't.

All over the world, professionals spend thousands of dollars on building and maintaining websites without being able to answer one big question: What do you want your website to do?

Creating a website without a marketing strategy can be an expensive and time-consuming mistake. Here's an illustration from the simpler world of paper and postage. Imagine that you hired a graphic designer, printed 5,000 four-color tri-fold brochures, and when the boxes arrived, you asked yourself, "Gee, what shall I do with these?"

That scenario may sound a bit embarrassing as it stands, but let's take it further. Suppose the first idea that occurs to you is mailing your new brochure to a list of 500 names you collected by exhibiting at a trade show. But then you realize that you didn't have the brochure designed as a self-mailer — all six panels are filled with graphics and copy.

To mail your brochure, you will now need 500 envelopes. Of course, you want to use the ones printed with your address and logo, but how much do those cost apiece? And do you have 500 extra in stock? What will be the cost in money or time to get envelopes printed, addressed, and stuffed? How long will all this take? Was any of this in your budget when you had the brochures printed?

This brochure example can tell us much about what goes wrong in creating websites. Many sites are constructed to be simply electronic brochures. Professionals often get their sites designed by sending the same text they would use on a printed brochure to a web designer, and saying, "Put this on the web."

Here's what is wrong with that. If you want your website to attract traffic on its own, your website must be *designed* to attract traffic. Your design and content must be optimized for search engines, including factors like keyword selection, link popularity, and the ratio of useful content to promotional copy — all of which you may know nothing about.

You have a choice in designing your site and integrating it with your overall marketing strategy. You can choose to make your site an electronic brochure without content attractive to search engines built into the design. If you do this, you must direct traffic to your site by other means — advertise, promote, exhibit, speak, write, network, mail, call, etc.

> If you're going to spend all the time and money to build a website, doesn't it make sense to have the site bring you clients, rather than you having to bring clients to the site?

Unfortunately, many professionals find this out after the fact. They put up the site and then slowly realize that no one is seeing it. So, they start spending time and money on pay-per-click listings, social media ads, online directories, email blasts, postcards, and more.

An alternative is to design your site to attract traffic in the first place. If you're going to spend all the time and money to build a website, doesn't it make sense to have the site bring you clients, rather than you having to bring clients to the site?

To create a high-traffic website, it must be search-engine friendly. Over 60% of all website traffic comes from search engines. When a client types in a keyword phrase you hope will bring them to you, your site needs to be one of the top 10 results shown or most searchers will never find you. To earn top positions in the major search engines, you or your web designer must know the guidelines the engines use to create their rankings, and mold your site to meet them.

Some of these guidelines relate to the content of your site, and how it is written and organized. Others have to do with the technical details of how your site is constructed. Still more are related to the nature and quantity of other sites who link their site to yours. If you don't want to know these specifics, you'd better hire someone who does. That's the problem with letting just anyone who labels themselves a web designer create a site for you.

Looking at a design firm's portfolio of completed sites will tell you only a small part of what you need to know about the firm's abilities. Who wrote the content for those sites? Who chose the keyword phrases to be emphasized? Who designed the page layout and navigation? And here's a key question: what did the designer do to make those sites search-engine friendly?

To create an attractive, useful website that will attract traffic and generate paying clients requires a four-way combination of design ability, technical expertise, marketing know-how, and search engine savvy. You know which of these capabilities you already have, and what new skills you're willing to learn. Make sure you hire people who have the rest.

MARKETING ALONG THE
PATH OF LEAST RESISTANCE

❖

Do you find sales and marketing to often be a struggle? It doesn't have to be that way. The most successful professionals make it look easy because they have found a way to market themselves that is effortless. Perhaps you have tried to copy what those successful people were doing, and it didn't work for you. Here's why.

Marketing is not a one-size-fits-all endeavor. You have to find your own unique path, the one that works best for you and your business. To make marketing and selling easy, that path needs to be the one where you will encounter the least resistance — both from the marketplace and from inside yourself.

Here are six steps to put you on the road to effortless sales and marketing.

1. Be willing to let go of struggle. You may believe you want sales and marketing to be easier, but stop and think for a moment. Is there a part of you that is so used to things being difficult that you continue allowing them to be an uphill climb? Is it secretly gratifying somehow to work so hard? Whenever you find yourself struggling about marketing, pause and ask yourself, "How could this be easier?"

2. Market to the people you like, and who like you. A colleague once told me I would never earn a living marketing my services to small businesses. "You have to focus on getting corporate clients," she said. "Then you can afford to work with entrepreneurs once in a while."

33

Thank goodness I didn't listen to her. Maybe that was the formula that worked for her business, but it wasn't a match for what I wanted at all. One of the reasons I became self-employed was to spend more time working outside corporate environments. If I had followed her advice, I would have failed miserably.

3. Start with the people who are ready for your message. Yes, there is a population out there who would hire you if only you could make them understand what you offer and how you can help them. Educating those people can become part of your long-term mission. But in the meantime, you have bills to pay.

> If you persist in marketing to people who can't pay your fees, you will encounter not just resistance, but a brick wall.

Seek out the clients who are most likely to already understand the value of what you do. If you are a money manager, you'll gain more clients by speaking at the Millionaires Circle than you would at either the Chamber of Commerce or the Small Business Administration. On the other hand, if you consult with corporations on reducing their carbon footprint, you'll get better results by networking with Businesses for the Environment than you would with the Millionaires Circle.

4. Choose marketing strategies that match who you are. I'll be the first to admit that I'm a mediocre cold caller. It just doesn't fit my personal style. So, I focus on the strategies that are natural to me — speaking, writing, and networking to build referrals. I've consistently maintained a thriving business that way for over twenty-five years now.

One of my clients is a business coach who targets small businesses and professional service firms. Her market is identical to mine, but her personality is completely different. She loves to cold call, and has been able to fill her practice that way. Speaking and networking don't come naturally to her at all. It's a good thing she didn't try to copy me.

5. Find people who can pay what you need to charge. If you persist in marketing to people who can't pay your fees, you will encounter not just resistance, but a brick wall. Don't give up because it seems that no one in the population you want to serve has any money. You need to look for an intersection between your desired market and people who have enough resources to hire you.

Colleagues have told me many times that one-person businesses in start-up mode can't or won't pay for business coaching. But I have had many, many people in this situation as full-fee clients. The intersection is that these folks were high net worth individuals before becoming entrepreneurs. People say you can't make money working with public schools, but I have had clients who do so as consultants, workshop leaders, and speakers. An intersection they have found is schools with funds obtained from grants and corporate sponsors.

6. Pay attention to how people respond when you talk about your business. A client of mine used to be a computer skills trainer with corporate clients. When she talked about her work, people nodded politely. But what she really wanted to do was teach public speaking. When she began to talk about that idea, her listeners got excited.

The difference wasn't in the content of her message —
public speaking can be just as dry a topic as how to use
computer software. It was her own enthusiasm for the work
that attracted such a positive response. If you really want your
marketing to be effortless, you need to be in a business that
excites *you*.

WHEN TO TOOT YOUR OWN HORN

❖

Every day in your business, something happens that people should know about. Perhaps you get booked to speak, or you begin reaching out to a new type of customer, or you have an article published. Yet most of the time, the only people aware of these significant events are those you are interacting with to make it happen, and you.

We might chuckle at the artist or performer who is waiting to be "discovered," but self-employed professionals are often just as guilty of hanging back when there's a bit of self-promotion to be done. Consider the following examples of ideal occasions for informing your clients, prospects, referral sources, and maybe even the media, that you have done something special:

- Having a guest blog post or article published
- Winning an award or competition
- Being elected or appointed to office in a professional or civic organization
- Obtaining an important new client, contract, or strategic alliance
- Giving noteworthy service to an existing client
- Opening or relocating your office
- Expanding to serve a new market
- Offering a new product, service, or seminar
- Launching a new or redesigned website, blog, or social media channel
- Reporting an invention or discovery
- Expressing a unique opinion on a topical subject
- Being selected to speak at a meeting or conference
- Completing a survey or study
- Publishing a case study, white paper, or ebook

- Being quoted or mentioned in the media or blogosphere
- Landing an interview on radio, TV, a podcast, or web radio

> ...significant happenings give you a reason to stay in touch with people, remind them of your value, and build your credibility as a qualified professional.

Whenever an event like this occurs, take advantage of the opportunity to notify everyone on your mailing list and in your personal network. These significant happenings give you a reason to stay in touch with people, remind them of your value, and build your credibility as a qualified professional.

Don't be shy; share your news in as many places as possible. If you're invited to speak at an industry conference, for example, you might announce it in a number of different ways:

- Post your announcement as a social media status update.
- Send your clients, hot prospects, and top referral sources an email with your announcement and a link to the conference website.
- Mention the conference and your presentation topic in your next newsletter.
- Announce your upcoming appearance in a blog entry, or your website's home page or calendar page, or on your social media business page.
- Include the conference brochure when you mail invoices to your clients, and add a personal note inviting them to join you there.

- Put a copy of the conference brochure in your marketing kit.
- Post an announcement to online communities you belong to (when posting guidelines permit).
- Send a notice to your professional association for the member news section of their newsletter or website.

Some new developments in your business will be newsworthy enough to reach beyond your own network and inform the media in your local community or industry. If you believe your event might be of interest to news outlets, issue a one-page press release describing what has occurred, and include your opinion about the event.

For example, if you win an award, describe how you feel about winning. If you are elected to office, outline your goals for the organization. It will add to your credibility if the event you're reporting is also acknowledged by someone else. When reporting on a new strategic alliance, for example, include a quote from your alliance partner about its significance to his/her organization.

When you do appear in the media, no matter how small the mention, be sure to capitalize on it. Unless you are on the cover of a major publication or featured on national TV, don't expect many people to contact you as a result of your appearance alone.

Instead, use your media appearance as another reason to let people know about your success. With print stories, published articles, or online mentions, make copies for your marketing kit, and use them as handouts at speaking engagements and trade shows. Frame them and hang them on the wall of your office. With online stories, post a link to the piece on social media and your website, and mention it in your newsletter or blog.

When you land a live interview on radio, TV, or online, let everyone in your network know when you will be appearing. After it takes place, let them know how it went. You will quickly discover that you'll often land more business as a result of telling people about your interview that you will from the interview itself!

You may be hesitant about broadcasting your achievements at first. It might feel like you are showing off, or you may worry how people will react. But you'll quickly find that your clients and colleagues actually want to hear news from you, as long as you don't constantly barrage them with it. People who do business with you or send you referrals will want to know when you have something new to offer. When you have a major success, they'll wish to congratulate you.

When you share valuable expertise in an article, interview, or speaking engagement, people in your network will be eager to learn what you have to say. When your story is truly newsworthy, local media outlets, your professional association, and your industry's trade press will want to hear about it. And your prospective clients would much rather receive an invitation, article, or announcement with useful information than one more sales letter or brochure.

So, don't keep your successes a secret, or wait for someone else to discover how talented you are. Start spreading the word. Telling more people about the good things that are happening in your world will increase your visibility, boost your credibility, and create ongoing demand for your professional services.

THE THREE "R"S
OF PROFESSIONAL SERVICES MARKETING

❖

At certain months of the year, many self-employed professionals feel an urge to go "back to school." Even when you haven't attended a class in years, it's habitual for the end of summer, close of the holiday season, or a return from vacation to suggest you should be paying less attention to family and fun and more to making a living.

When it's time for you to turn your focus to business, consider how you might incorporate into your back-to-business agenda the back-to-basics curriculum of the Three "R"s of professional services marketing: relationship, referral, and reach.

1. Relationship: The cornerstone of every self-employed professional's marketing strategy should be relationship-building. If a marketing tactic you're considering contributes to stronger relationships between you and your prospects, it's worthy of your attention. If it doesn't, think twice before using it, and certainly don't rely on it.

Marketing that can lead to better relationships includes activities like lunch and coffee dates, giving educational talks, publishing valuable content online and in print, and personal exchanges via phone, email, or social media.

Marketing that rarely leads to better relationships — and can sometimes damage them — includes phone calls, letters, and emails focused on hype about your services, subscribing people to newsletters and email broadcasts they never requested, and besieging your social networking contacts with promotional announcements.

Don't be misled by advice pushing the flavor of the week in marketing. If a new tactic suggested to you isn't relationship-oriented, it probably isn't worth your time.

2. Referral: Prospects who come to you by way of a referral are more likely to become clients than those who you connect with in almost any other way. They have often already decided to work with you when you hear from them, and are less likely to question your rates or your expertise.

> ...you do have to reach out rather than simply wait and react, even though outreach is often more uncomfortable.

Generating more referrals, then, should be an essential component of your marketing. Instead of expending most of your effort on filling the pipeline with unknown prospects and making cold approaches, spend more time cultivating relationships with likely referral sources.

Many professionals mistakenly believe that if they simply provide good service to their clients, the referrals that naturally result will be enough. But this is rarely the case. The best referrals often come from people who have never been your clients — members of your trade association or networking group, other professionals who serve your market, and centers of influence in your community. Time spent getting to know these folks better can be much more productive than approaching strangers.

3. Reach: Clients don't appear just because you are there waiting for them. You have to reach out. In marketing, reach takes many different forms — for example, you reaching out to people you already know to build better relationships, you reaching out to new potential referral sources, and you reaching outside your comfort zone to have personal interactions with prospects.

The point is that you do have to reach out rather than simply wait and react, even though outreach is often more uncomfortable. It's tempting to rely on build-it-and-they-will-come marketing like websites consisting solely of promo copy, or online "networking" with people you don't even know, or pay-per-click ads, or directory listings. And there are plenty of vendors doing their own outreach to sell you on these approaches so you don't even have to go looking for them.

But if it was really that easy to get clients — just launch a website, say, or buy an ad, and you'll have all the clients you need — why haven't all the folks selling you these strategies retired to tropical islands by now?

As far as marketing tactics go, if it sounds too good to be true, it probably is. So, get back to basics with your marketing. Build relationships, cultivate referrals, and reach out proactively to prospects and referral sources rather than waiting for them to find you. With the Three "R"s as your guide, you'll have everything you need to go to the head of the class.

INFORMATION IS THE PRESENT; CONNECTION IS THE FUTURE

❖

How many times already today has someone tried to sell you something? The ads come in by email, text, postal mail, fax, radio, magazines, newspapers, TV, social media, and your web browser; the salespeople write, call, and approach you in the store or showroom. Are you even paying attention any more? How often do you actually buy something because someone you didn't know tried to sell it to you?

> *"What consumers are primarily interested in today are not features, but relationships."*
> — **Harry Beckwith,** *Selling the Invisible*

Your clients — consumers and businesses alike — are just like you. They are not only fed up with hype, most of the time they don't even see it. Overwhelmed with communications, they tune out the vast majority of the marketing messages they are presented with, just in order to get through their day. After attending a race plastered with Coca-Cola logos, a survey revealed that only a third of the attendees could remember who the corporate sponsor was.

> *"A weekday edition of The New York Times contains more information than the average person was likely to come across in a lifetime in 17th-century England."*
> — **R.S. Wurman,** *Information Anxiety*

Making information available to your clients is still important, so don't take down your website or throw out your brochures. But with so many communications arriving all the time, your clients want control over how and when they receive your information. More than ever before, people want to do business with people they know, like, and trust.

As the principal of a service business, what you are really marketing is you, not the service. When you are the product, your customers need to know who you are. They want to feel a connection with you, and know that they can trust you, before they will consider doing business with you.

"Beleaguered by email spam and intrusive pop-up ads on the Internet, consumers are using the 'delete' button with increasing frequency and losing confidence in other traditional forms of advertising as well... Consumers rank word-of-mouth recommendations from others as the most trusted form of advertising."
— PlanetFeedback.com

According to psychologists, a primary motivational factor for human behavior is affiliation, defined as "the desire to establish and maintain warm and friendly relations with others." We are naturally drawn toward experiences where affiliation is possible, and avoid situations where it is not.

When we receive a recommendation from someone we are already affiliated with, we believe that following that recommendation will continue the positive experience. If we think developing an affiliation is possible with someone new because they have approached us in a warm and friendly way, we are encouraged to establish a new relationship, whether it is personal or business.

"With the amount of information presented increasing, mass marketing campaigns become less effective… One-to-one marketing will not just be a possibility, it will be a necessity."
— **Easton Consultants,** *Information Overload*

Establishing a one-to-one connection with your prospective customers can begin with projecting the warm and friendly image that encourages affiliation. Make yourself available for contact and conversation that isn't necessarily leading directly to a sale. Encourage word of mouth by developing and keeping in touch with a network of current and former clients, colleagues, competitors, referral partners, and influential people.

> Focus on providing information to clients in objective, rather than promotional ways.

Focus on providing information to clients in objective, rather than promotional ways. One study found that a commercial website scored 27% higher in "usability" by visitors when written in an objective style (sharing information) instead of a promotional style (singing the company's praises). You can carry this principle offline by writing helpful articles and giving talks in preference to sending brochures and making cold calls.

Participate in your client community as a peer by attending conferences, seminars, fundraisers, and other educational and social events. On the web, take part in conversations via social media and online forums. When you read articles and blog posts, take a moment to post your comments to the author where other visitors can see them.

Prospective buyers name newsletters, blogs, and other forms of opt-in, reader-friendly communications as one of their most trusted sources of information about products and services. As well as publishing one of these yourself, it pays to be mentioned in someone else's.

"Get to know the influentials… invite them in and engage them in a conversation… Most are local community leaders, or have real involvement in their communities, and as such are the nodes of wide personal networks. They are the people… to whom others look for advice or counsel."
— **Edward Keller and Jonathan Berry,** ***The Influentials***

When you engage in a community, people begin to know you from the words of others instead of from your words alone. You can even create your own community by starting an affinity group or business network, launching a group on social media, hosting an online forum or live conference, inviting comments on your website, posting reader responses in your newsletter, and much more.

The real key is to begin connecting in person with the population you want to reach, instead of relying on promotion and selling to bring them to you and make them want to buy.

WHAT YOU ARE MARKETING IS YOURSELF
❖

"Call us today and change your life," proclaimed the hot pink flyer on the bulletin board. It was signed "Sunrise Hypnotherapy" with a phone number and a blind email address. No practitioner's name appeared anywhere on the flyer.

Posted near it were numerous other leaflets, advertising everything from life coaching to bookkeeping. Fully two-thirds of the flyers I spotted were similarly anonymous. Some displayed a business name; others simply described the service, e.g., "acupuncture." But the names of the people offering many of these services were curiously absent.

I had to wonder if these nameless flyers ever produced a single phone call. It seems to me that if you are going to trust someone to change your life, you would like to know a little about them first.

Surfing the web, I discovered the same baffling omission on the websites of numerous self-employed professionals. Professionals targeting the corporate market seemed to be just as likely to conceal their identity as those oriented toward consumers. Management consultants, executive coaches, and seminar leaders alike were promoting their one-person businesses by mentioning only their company names, and referring to themselves in the plural as "we" and "us."

If I were searching for a professional to help my company solve a problem, I would be pretty skeptical of an individual who identified him or herself only as "Exegesis Management Group." If I'm going to consider hiring a consultant, coach, or trainer, a good starting place would be knowing the professional's name.

Where are the people behind these offerings? Why have they decided to cloak their identities and promote an anonymous business instead of their talented, experienced selves? What misguided or outdated advice are they following that makes them believe this is an effective way to market their professional services?

Marketing a service business is not the same as marketing a product. Potential buyers of your service don't have the same opportunity to touch, taste, or test drive what you offer as they do when buying a tomato or a car. To spend hundreds or thousands of dollars on a service they can't sample in advance, your prospects must be able to trust you. And to build their trust, they must get to know you.

> To spend hundreds or thousands of dollars on a service they can't sample in advance, your prospects must... get to know you.

Examine your website, brochure, or flyer with a critical eye. Does your name appear prominently on the first page? Is there a bio of you in an obvious location that describes your credentials and experience? What about a photo? If visitors or readers want to get to know you better before contacting you personally, do you offer them options like a blog, newsletter, articles you've published, videos of you, or your speaking schedule?

If your firm has more than one principal who provides services, identify them all. If the business is really just you, but you bring in subcontractors as needed, that anonymous "we" in your marketing copy isn't fooling anyone. Feature yourself as the company founder and describe your expertise. Identify some of your subcontractors by name and give their backgrounds, so clients can see who they might be working with.

Perhaps you have unconsciously been copying the marketing style used by large consulting firms, seminar companies, and national service providers in industries like financial services or health care. These well-known companies rely on building their brand to attract new customers by promoting the organization as a whole, instead of the individuals within it. But these firms spend millions of dollars and take years to build those reputations. You don't have that kind of money or time to spare.

The strongest asset you have in marketing your business is actually yourself. Providing visible evidence of your experience, credentials, and capabilities is what will ultimately convince skeptical buyers that you are the right person for the job. Allowing them to get to know you will build their trust.

You deserve to be the star of your own promotional materials. So, stop hiding behind an anonymous marketing image and let your customers know how talented you really are.

FIVE MYTHS OF INTERNET MARKETING
FOR SELF-EMPLOYED PROFESSIONALS

❖

There's more marketing hype published on the Internet in one day than P.T. Barnum generated in his lifetime. Like a worm swallowing its tail, the Internet marketing beast feeds mostly on itself. The vast majority of what appears on the Internet about marketing is designed to help you market products and services sold and delivered exclusively on the Internet.

So, what does that mean for the self-employed professional whose web presence is primarily aimed at selling his or her own services? You know, services delivered the old-fashioned way, by humans interacting face-to-face or at least voice-to-voice. At best, the average professional is likely to be overwhelmed by the sheer volume of online marketing advice available. At worst, he or she is being seriously misled by it.

The problem is that marketing your own professional services is simply not the same as marketing a retail product or an anonymous business service. You can't sell management consulting like you do web hosting; nor can you sell executive coaching the same way you do an ebook. If you try to market yourself by following advice designed for marketing Internet products and services, you're likely to make some serious mistakes.

Here are five Internet marketing myths that may be hazardous to the health of your business.

Myth #1: It all starts with a great website. Actually, the place where it starts is with a well-defined service. If you don't have a crystal-clear picture of who you are marketing to and exactly what you're selling them, the best website in the world won't get you clients. Before you even think about building a website, you should know who your target market is, how to describe your professional specialty, and what specific benefits your work provides for your clients.

The content of your site is much more important than the design. Yes, you should have a professional-looking site, but a brilliant design and dazzling graphics won't pay off anywhere near as well as a clear explanation of why a client should work with you. Useful material such as articles, assessments, and other samples of your expertise will go much further to persuade prospective clients than flash intros and interactive menus.

Myth #2: More traffic translates to increased profits. The only result that more traffic to your website guarantees you is increased bandwidth use on your web hosting account. Before spending money on banner ads, pay-per-click listings, or search engine optimization to drive more visitors to your site, you need to be sure that they'll want to do business with you once they get there.

> Hype-laden web copy may be effective in selling info-products or home-study courses, but it hardly inspires trust.

Ask your colleagues and current clients to critique the content of your site. Do they understand what you offer? Can they see concrete benefits to your target audience? Revise your site's content based on their feedback. Then personally invite some prospective clients to visit and touch base afterward. Do your prospects seem more inclined to do business with you after seeing your site? If so, you're on the right track. If not, you still have work to do.

Myth #3: Do whatever it takes to build your list. There's no question that a substantial opt-in mailing list is a valuable marketing asset, but the quality of names on your list is much more important than the quantity. Acquiring names through giveaways of other people's material, trading lists with joint venture partners, or purchasing them from a vendor rarely provides qualified buyers truly interested in your services.

Absolutely, ask your site visitors and people you meet to join your email list and offer them something of value in return. A well-written report, helpful ebook, or informative audio can all be effective premiums. But, your premium should be directly related to the services you provide and also serve to increase your professional credibility. Names acquired from promotional gimmicks or unknown sources seldom turn into paying clients.

Myth #4: Killer copy is the secret to sales. Hype-laden web copy may be effective in selling info-products or home-study courses, but it hardly inspires trust. You're not going to convince anyone to hire you as a consultant, coach, trainer, designer, or financial advisor by offering "not one, not two, but three valuable bonuses" as if you were selling steak knives on late-night TV.

Your Internet marketing persona should reflect the same professionalism as the work you do with your clients. If writing marketing copy isn't your forté, by all means hire a copywriting pro. But be sure you hire one with experience writing for professionals like yourself. The words on your site should inspire feelings of confidence about your abilities, and communicate your reliability and solid qualifications.

Myth #5: Just follow the winning formula and you will get rich. There's only one surefire recipe for Internet wealth I know of, and that's the business of selling surefire recipes. There seems to be an infinite number of buyers for every new get-rich-online scheme that is invented, but paradoxically, a precious few people successfully making money online.

The Internet may be a different medium for marketing professional services than traditional approaches like making calls, writing letters, or meeting people in person, but the same time-honored principles still apply. There is no winning formula for overnight success. The secret to landing clients remains what it always has been — build relationships and get people to know, like, and trust you.

If your website, blog, social media presence, and other Internet-based activities contribute to building long-term, trusting relationships with prospective clients and referral sources, you'll get business on the web. But if you blast your message out to anyone who will listen, aiming for a quick profit, the Internet won't bring you any more business than standing on a street corner with a megaphone.

SEVEN WAYS TO BUILD
MARKETING RELATIONSHIPS

❖

"Relationship marketing." "Word-of-mouth advertising." "The future of marketing is one-to-one." "People like to do business with people they know, like, and trust." You've likely heard these adages before. But what does it really mean to build relationships with people in order to sell something?

Does it work to make personal connections with a hidden agenda? How do you go about creating relationships for marketing purposes without feeling sleazy? Here are seven tips for building marketing relationships you can feel good about.

1. Start with the best audience. When you choose the right target market for your business, relationship-building becomes an enjoyable process. Your ideal clients and referral sources are people you already enjoy spending time with. Your clients should be people whose goals and problems you care about; your referral partners should be those who share your concerns for the welfare of the client base you serve.

If you feel uncomfortable when you approach business contacts with the aim of getting to know them better, gauge your personal interest level in making the connection. A lack of interest on your part may be a signal that you are reaching out to the wrong group of people. Relationship marketing will not be a success for you if you don't have a sincere concern and a feeling of affinity for your prospective clients.

2. Treat prospects like clients and referral sources like friends. The best business relationships go beyond superficiality. When interacting with prospective clients, treat them as if they were paying clients already. Listen carefully to their issues and respond thoughtfully. Share your ideas with them and ask for their opinions. Instead of pressing for a sale, open a dialogue so the two of you can become better acquainted.

Socializing with your prospects and referral sources can allow relationships to build on more levels than just discussing how and when to do business. Lunch or coffee meetings may be the most obvious choices for social encounters, but consider others as well: a walk in the park, a game of tennis, a picnic with your families, or attending a concert, lecture, or art show together.

> Giving prospective clients a taste of what you can provide builds their trust and demonstrates your competence.

3. Offer resources and solutions with no strings attached. Giving prospective clients a taste of what you can provide builds their trust and demonstrates your competence. It also gives them opportunities to interact with you more frequently.

When prospects tell you about a need, suggest solutions even if the answer doesn't involve hiring you. Offer free information on your website and at speaking engagements in the form of articles, special reports, resource directories, or assessment tools. The more you are perceived as a resource, the more clients will welcome repeated contacts with you, and your relationship with them will grow.

4. Tell the truth. Hidden agendas and ulterior motives will sabotage your relationship-building efforts. The people you try to connect with will sense your insincerity and your attempts will backfire. Also, you're likely to be uncomfortable with the idea of misrepresenting your intentions. If you aren't comfortable with what you are doing, you won't market yourself well.

Don't try to conceal your purpose when building relationships in the hope of landing new clients or referrals. Come right out and tell people your intent. For example, "I'd like to have you as a client some day. Perhaps for now I can provide some resources or suggestions regarding your current situation at no charge. Then as we get to know each other better, we can see whether it would make sense for us to work together at some point."

5. Discover multiple ways to connect. One-on-one meetings aren't the only way to deepen relationships. It's often easier to get to know people in group settings. Many lasting bonds form because people volunteer together on a community project, meet regularly as part of a networking group, or participate in the same online community.

Seek out two or three places where people in your target market seem to gather and make yourself at home there. Join a task force or committee, or take on an active role where you will meet other members, such as newsletter editor, program chair, or discussion group moderator.

6. Continue to stay in touch over time. You can't build a relationship once and assume it will stay alive. People need to hear from you and about you regularly.

Think beyond phone calls and coffee dates to keep in touch with your relationship pool. Publishing a newsletter or blog can help you to stay connected with a large number of people who already know you. Active participation in an online community can do the same. Brief personal notes also go a long way, especially when attached to useful information like an article or event invitation. When the article or event is your own, adding a note personalizes the communication.

7. Rely on your personal strengths. We all prefer to connect with others in different ways. If chatting on the phone isn't natural behavior for you, you may want to use email, social media, one-to-one meetings, or group gatherings as more comfortable ways of relationship-building. If you find business lunches awkward, consider meeting people in more casual settings like a city park or the beach.

Building relationships is a natural human activity. If you're finding that building relationships for business purposes feels unnatural, you might be copying someone else's style instead of finding your own. Cultivating relationships should give you a positive feeling rather than a negative one. And the better you feel about doing it, the more relationship-building you will do.

ARE YOU SABOTAGING
YOUR OWN MARKETING?

❖

Most self-employed professionals work hard at marketing their businesses, but far too many don't succeed as well as they could. Unfortunately, some of the hardest-working self-marketers sometimes sabotage their own efforts. By making one or more common mistakes in how you approach marketing your business, you may be throwing away a considerable amount of precious time and hard-earned money.

Here are seven ways you may be sabotaging your own marketing, and how to get it back on track.

1. You're doing plenty of marketing, but almost no selling. For a self-employed professional, marketing and selling often blend into each other rather than being clearly distinct activities. So, it's not always obvious when selling gets left out of the equation. Think of marketing as everything you do to get a prospective client to call you, email you, or respond when you initiate contact. Selling is what needs to happen once you and the client actually connect. Without that live connection, selling can't ever happen.

In a typical selling exchange, you ask your prospects exactly what they need, then explain specifically how you can help. At some point, you ask for their commitment to move forward, and that's when a sale takes place. For most self-employed professionals, having an interactive conversation like this is an essential step in getting someone to hire you. The primary goal of your marketing, then, should always be to convince people to have that conversation with you.

Don't be misled by online marketing gurus who suggest that your website copy should do all the selling for you. That approach may work to sell ebooks or home-study courses, but it doesn't do the job for selling professional services. Every marketing strategy you use should ultimately result in your having more live conversations with prospective clients. If it doesn't, you're probably wasting your time.

2. You're attending networking events or giving talks, but not following up afterwards. A professional's life would be so much simpler if prospects would just walk up to you at an event and say, "I'd like to become your client." But that's a pretty rare occurrence. Ninety-nine percent of the time, the sale takes place in a follow-up conversation after the fact. And more often than not, it takes multiple follow-up contacts to get to that point.

> ...never assume that a prospect remembers who you are or what you do, even if you spoke with him or her just the week before.

When you attend, or speak at, an event, plan in advance to spend at least twice as much time following up with those you met as you spent at the original event. That's where the real payoff from networking or speaking comes from. Whenever you hear professionals say that networking or speaking "didn't work" for them, you can almost bet that it's because they were expecting to see results just from attending.

3. You're following up with prospects without making a clear offer. You can never assume that a prospect remembers who you are or what you do, even if you spoke with him or her just the week before. Following up to see if prospects are ready to move forward will get you nowhere if they still don't understand how you can help them. Every time you make contact, re-introduce yourself with your full name and profession or tag line, and remind your prospect of your last conversation.

Get specific about how you can help. Instead of simply saying you are a graphic designer, tell prospects you create logos, business cards, and brochures. Rather than just calling yourself a communications consultant or business writer, offer to assist with employee newsletters, annual reports, or ghostwriting articles. Even when you don't know what a prospect's exact needs are, giving examples will help you better communicate how you can be of service.

4. You're building traffic to your website, but not capturing visitors once they arrive. Just as with all other forms of marketing, more sales on the web take place after a period of follow-up than ever occur on a prospect's first visit to your website. If all your website says is, "please hire me now," you'll lose out on the opportunity to follow up with your visitors, and much of your traffic will go to waste.

Give your first-time visitors a reason to stay in touch with you by offering a free newsletter or blog to subscribe to, a complimentary white paper or assessment to download (in return for their email address), or a low-cost ebook or audio to introduce them to your work. Then follow up at regular intervals with more useful information and reminders about how you can be of service.

5. You often delay a day or two before responding to prospect inquiries. Even when you're busy, when a prospect contacts you, respond quickly. Keep in mind that when prospects are ready to hire an accountant, or career coach, or web designer, they may be contacting your competitors at the same time they contact you. The first professional who returns the call or email is often the one who gets the business. Don't lose out on all the effort you put into getting someone to contact you just by not responding to them promptly.

6. You have an outgoing voice mail or email message implying you're too busy to respond. A surefire way to discourage new clients is to make them think you're already too busy. Clients don't want to work with a professional who is overloaded with other commitments. If your outgoing voice mail message says you are offsite until Friday and will be returning calls then, prospects may simply hang up rather than leave a message. If your email autoresponse says you won't be checking email this week, your prospects' next email may be to your competition.

Occasional absences (and much-needed vacations) are a necessity of business, but think twice about the impact of frequent out-of-office messages on prospective clients. Use a virtual assistant or answering service to screen messages when you are unavailable and make sure new inquiries reach you promptly. Or use a voice mail provider with a "find me" option to forward calls to your cell phone.

7. Every time someone hears from you, you're offering something different. One of the most important factors in convincing a prospect to hire a professional is the level of trust he or she has in you. One of the best ways to build trust is by communicating a consistent message. Conveniently, this same approach also builds familiarity and name recognition. Hearing the same message repeatedly helps us remember the person delivering it, and start to feel like we know him or her.

Don't feel as if you need to change what or how you are marketing just because prospects don't respond the first time you approach them. You are more likely to build the trust and recognition that will eventually lead to a sale by continuing to deliver the same basic message than by trying out a new one each time. It's fine to offer chocolate one time and vanilla another, as long as what you are selling is still ice cream. But don't suddenly switch to offering cake instead.

Self-sabotage in marketing is all too frequent among self-employed professionals, but you don't have to be a victim of mistakes like these. If you feel as if you've been working too hard at marketing without seeing enough results, stop for a moment and see if the reason could possibly be something you are doing to harm yourself.

ONLINE TOOLS FOR MARKETING: FRIEND OR FOE?

❖

Every self-employed professional should have a website, an ezine or blog, an email marketing strategy, and a social media presence, right? If you're not taking maximum advantage of online technology to market your professional services, you are behind the times, and missing out on huge opportunities. At least that's what most marketing experts would have you believe. But how valid is this advice? And is it for everyone?

Look at newsletters, for example. Before email was widely available, newsletters were printed on paper and sent by mail. There's no question that email is a more economical solution for sending a newsletter. Instead of being able to afford only a few hundred newsletters at a cost of $1 or more each, you can send tens of thousands for only pennies. With an ezine, technology can save you money and allow you to extend your marketing reach. This is one of the many ways that online technology can be your friend. Here are some others:

- Your website can attract new customers to your business from across the street or far outside your local area. If your site has high Google rankings for keywords prospective clients might search for, you may get dozens of inquiries from people who otherwise would never hear of you.
- Using email autoresponders can help you automate your follow-up with likely prospects. Just subscribe a prospect to an autoresponder list once, then send periodic broadcasts to the whole list, encouraging prospects to hire you or attend your events.

- Being active on social media or online communities can allow you to network with a large group of people in your target market without leaving your home or office. Appearing on webinars or live chats permits you to be a public speaker without the time and expense of travel, and speak to national or global audiences.

For these reasons and more, it appears that using online technology is an affordable way to reach prospective clients easily. You can potentially attract larger numbers of prospects for fewer dollars than with many more traditional methods of outreach. But there are pitfalls.

Broadcast email can be an efficient solution for following up with prospects who already know about you. But it's a terrible way to introduce yourself to a prospect for the first time.

> Broadcast email can be an efficient solution for following up with prospects who already know about you. But it's a terrible way to introduce yourself to a prospect for the first time.

Far too many self-employed professionals add subscribers to their ezine or broadcast email lists without their permission. Not only is this ineffective as a marketing strategy — since most readers simply delete email from people they don't recognize — but it can seriously backfire when someone is offended by your unsolicited mail.

Here are some other ways that using online tools for marketing can become your foe.

Being online makes it easy to hide. When you have a web and social media presence, an ezine or blog, and use email to contact your customers, you may think there's no reason to contact them in person. You may feel justified in not picking up the phone, attending a business event, or suggesting a lunch date if you think your technology is doing the job for you.

But a website or email isn't an equivalent substitute for a prospect hearing your voice or seeing your face. It's pretty rare for someone to hire a professional without talking to him or her first, so if you put off the talking, you may also be putting off the hiring.

Launching and maintaining an attractive and useful website or blog, and achieving high search engine rankings for it, can be an expensive and time-consuming activity. You can easily find yourself expending much more effort to land each client than you would ever pay using offline marketing methods.

A high-traffic website or blog is a valuable resource for a business that can take advantage of a global presence or a large volume of new clients. But if your business is primarily local or you only need a few new clients each year, you may end up working hard to achieve a level of visibility you don't really need.

Too many inquiries from the web can waste your time. Anonymous visitors to your site will often email to ask about prices and other details. These inquiries are completely unqualified — you don't know anything about the people who are writing. If you take the time for a thorough reply to each one, they can consume a significant amount of energy.

On the web as well as off, prospects who are referred to you by people who know your work are much more likely to hire you than those who find you by accident. Since that's so, perhaps it makes sense to put more effort into building referrals than into building a broader web presence.

Online technology is little different than any other method of marketing your services, in that you must judge how appropriate each strategy is for your unique circumstances.

If you find writing to be a chore, a regular ezine or blog is probably not the best choice for you. If you only need a few large, local clients each year, you may want a simple website for prospects to explore after you make contact with them, but not spend your time and money on search engine optimization, directory listings, or pay-per-click ads. Autoresponder reminders may be effective to increase enrollment in public workshops, but not such a good idea to sell in-house training to corporations.

Just because a strategy is the latest and greatest doesn't mean it's the best. Social media can be useful if your prospects frequently use these platforms for purposes related to your line of business, but not so good to reach people who limit their use of Facebook to keeping up with their kids, sign on to LinkedIn only when they're seeking their next job, and don't have a clue why anyone would ever use Twitter.

Relying completely on technology to bring in clients can also give you a false sense of productivity. When you are writing copy for your website or posting to social media, you feel like you are taking action about marketing. And these activities can be important behind the scenes steps, but you shouldn't confuse them with direct outreach to prospective clients. Web copy and social media posts will have no effect unless interested people actually read what you have written.

Online platforms provide just another set of marketing tools, not a complete solution. Using every marketing tool the web has to offer is not a requirement of doing business. The purpose of your marketing should be to bring you enough clients to earn the level of profit you desire. When online marketing tools add to your bottom line, they're worth employing. When they don't, there's no reason to use them.

STOP SELLING AND START SERVING
❖

"I don't like to sell." "Asking people for business makes me uncomfortable." "Selling feels manipulative and sleazy." "I'm good at what I do. Why don't clients just come to me?"

If any of these thoughts seem familiar, you may be stuck in an outdated perspective about selling that is holding back your success. Traditional sales models invoked adversarial images, as if selling were a battle between you and your prospects: "hook the customer," "convince prospects to buy," "overcome their objections," and "get past their resistance."

This variety of selling is rarely even taught any more, but the images persist, and unfortunately, so do some of the manipulative sales practices they represent. But just because you see them used doesn't mean they are effective. The reality is that being on the same side as your clients works much better than opposing them. And it's a lot more comfortable for you.

In fact, some of the most successful professionals in your field actually never "sell" at all. What they do instead is simply be of service.

A primary reason that people hire a professional services provider like you is to serve as an expert resource. Your clients count on you for guidance, advice, support, resources, contacts, expertise, specialized techniques, access to technology, and up-to-the minute information. Every one of these elements is something you can begin to provide your prospects before they ever become paying clients.

By freely offering information, advice, and resources to people who have not yet decided to hire you, the need for any clash of wills between prospect and salesperson disappears. Instead of creating sales resistance, your generosity dissolves the barriers between you. Prospects begin to think of you as a trusted resource instead of a vendor who wants their business. You become the first person they think of in your field — for their own needs and referrals as well.

Making the shift from selling to serving requires changes in more than just how you ask for the business to close the sale. Your service attitude must begin with your first contact and pervade every aspect of your marketing. Here are some examples of the many ways you can substitute a service attitude for a sales approach in all of your interactions with prospective clients.

> As a service professional, what you excel at is serving, not selling. Doing what you do best allows you to shine.

In your brochure:
Selling approach — Five reasons to hire me as your accountant
Serving approach — Ten ways to save money on your taxes

On your website:
Selling — Download our free survey on the benefits of executive coaching
Serving — Download our free survey on best practices in leadership development

At your speaking engagements:
Selling — Give me your card if you would like to find out more about chiropractic
Serving — Give me your card and I will send you a free report on drug-free alternatives for back pain

In your blog or newsletter:
Selling — In my work with resolving workplace conflicts, I use a powerful model for diffusing messy situations
Serving — Here is a summary of the conflict resolution model I've developed and some tips for using it in your workplace

As an article or blog topic:
Selling — Why work with an interior designer?
Serving — Choosing a design theme for your living room

On the phone:
Selling — I'd like to introduce myself: I'm a change management consultant and I specialize in...
Serving — I understand your company is going through some changes and I'd like to see if I can provide any helpful insights

In your ads:
Selling — Call for a 15% discount on your first appointment
Serving — Call for a free subscription to our wellness bulletin

To a networking contact:
Selling — Here are the web design skills I can offer your clients
Serving — If any of your clients are having web design challenges, I'll be happy to provide some tips at no charge

What you'll notice about these examples is that they don't necessarily require you to do more about sales and marketing. If you have a good marketing plan in place, you can keep right on using it. The difference is that you begin to treat your prospects like clients from the first moment you contact them. Instead of reserving your expertise for only those who have paid your fee, you share it with everyone you can.

Am I suggesting you give your professional services away for free? Absolutely not. Writing ten tips for saving taxes is not the same as preparing a tax return at no charge. Offering a few minutes of free advice on the phone is quite different from entering into a consulting engagement without being paid.

What I am suggesting is that your prospective clients deserve as much consideration as the close friends and family for whom you probably provide this type of quick, easy help routinely. After all, those people are unlikely to ever pay you for your time. Prospective clients, on the other hand, will be eager to pay your fee once they get a taste of what you can do for them.

As a service professional, what you excel at is serving, not selling. Doing what you do best allows you to shine. You'll be more comfortable, your prospects will trust and respect you, and you will naturally be in contact with them more often. As a result, more prospects will become clients without either of you having to suffer through a sales presentation.

AM I DOING SOMETHING WRONG?
❖

My clients often ask me to help figure out what's wrong with their marketing. The first question I ask is how much marketing they've been doing, since many failures have more to do with quantity than quality. But assuming you've been sufficiently active at promoting yourself, here are some other ways in which your marketing might need fixing.

There are three areas you should examine — the package of services you are offering, your marketing strategies, and your sales methods. In order to market and sell effectively, your package of services should meet the following requirements:

1. You are offering something people believe that they need.
2. Your clients perceive the value of your services to be equivalent to the price you're charging.
3. Your services are available where and when clients need to use them.
4. Either there's plenty of business for everybody in your field, or your competitors have no overwhelming advantages.

When your package of services doesn't meet these requirements, improving your marketing strategies or selling skills won't be enough. You may need to revisit some of the basic premises of your business. Talk to your colleagues, clients, and others in your target market to find out more about what your desired clients need and how they want to receive it.

Depending on what you discover, the solution may lie in re-positioning your services against those of the competition, changing your pricing structure, or offering your services in an entirely different way than you have in the past. For example, if you've been asking for an hourly rate, you may find more buyers if you're willing to complete some projects for a fixed price.

Once your package of services is in good shape, the next set of potential problems may lie with your sales and marketing techniques. Your marketing strategies are everything you do to get in contact with a prospective customer and make them think positively about you. Your sales methods are the steps you take to turn that positive contact into a paying client.

These are some of the most common sales and marketing mistakes that consultants, professionals, and other service providers make.

Not choosing a target market. You can't market to everybody. There isn't enough time in the day or money in your bank account to reach out to everyone who could possibly hire you. If you choose a specific category of client who has a compelling need for your services (and who you enjoy working with), you can tailor your marketing message, and focus your strategies.

> If people can't understand what you do, they can't figure out if they need you. You must develop a clear, concise description of your services…

Relying on advertising. People rarely hire a professional from an ad, even one that's targeted to a specific publication. While advertising does build your visibility, it's often more expensive and less effective than other visibility-builders like writing articles and giving talks. If you write and speak for the same audiences to which you might advertise, you'll have the added benefit of increased credibility as an expert.

Broadcasting a fuzzy marketing message. If people can't understand what you do, they can't figure out if they need you. You must develop a clear, concise description of your services that can be understood by people who aren't familiar with your field.

Lack of follow-up. A single contact is rarely enough to make someone remember you. Find ways to keep in touch with prospective clients or referral sources on a regular basis. Follow-up contacts don't have to be phone calls. Sending personal notes by mail or email, sharing useful articles, inviting people to lunch or coffee, or publishing a blog or ezine are all effective follow-up techniques.

Failing to establish a clear path to the sale. At the end of every conversation or email exchange, be sure to spell out the next step for clients to take if they want to do business with you. If they're not yet ready to buy, suggest a meeting, tell them you'll call in a week, or ask if you can contact them again next month.

Expecting short-term results from long-term strategies. While networking with potential clients and referral sources is often the best marketing strategy there is, the results are rarely immediate. Don't give up on making contacts and following up because you don't get business right away.

Finally, be aware of the possibility that you may be doing everything right! It often takes many months to close each individual sale. Some clients can't use you right now, but may be eager to hire you next year. Others are very interested in going forward, but need time to get management approval or resolve money issues.

If you're offering the right package to the right clients, delivering a clear and consistent marketing message, and working hard to close every potential sale, the only missing element may be patience.

PART II

--- ❖ ---

WHERE DO YOU START?
BUILDING YOUR SYSTEM OR PLAN

MARKETING: YOU GOTTA HAVE A SYSTEM

❖

Being successful at marketing does not result from one brilliant idea. Nor does it follow from stringing together a random series of marketing activities, no matter how many different approaches you manage to use. To bring in a sustainable flow of business on a consistent basis, you gotta have a system.

With no system for marketing and sales, you have no priorities for where to focus. "What should I do first?" a new coaching client will often ask me. "I need to update my website, arrange speaking engagements, launch a Facebook page, follow up on leads I already have... I don't even know where to begin."

When you lack guidelines for managing your time and money, you can quickly overspend those precious resources. "I thought I would update just one thing on my LinkedIn profile," a colleague recently posted. "Three hours later, I was still working on it."

Without a system, you also have no framework for making choices. Does it make sense for you to hire the search engine optimization expert you just met? Or should you take that class you heard about on how to launch a blog? Or maybe you should join the networking group someone recently invited you to.

One more missing element in system-less marketing is consistency, a crucial factor in successful marketing. When you don't have a blueprint to guide you, it's too easy to neglect what should be ongoing tasks, like following up on your unreturned phone calls or emails, posting to your blog or social media page, or sending broadcasts to your email list.

Here's what should be included in a marketing and sales system:

1. **What result you wish to see.** Name a number of clients, prospects, appointments, dollars, or some other quantifiable target.

2. **What approaches you will use to achieve that result.** Choose a spot in the marketing/sales cycle where you will focus, and identify specific strategies to follow.

> We often resist systems and structures… But making use of an effective system can actually be freeing.

3. **Exactly what you will do to implement those approaches.** Make a list of tasks to perform and tools you need to create or acquire.

4. **When you will do those things.** Specify when you will begin and when you will have projects or tools completed.

5. **How often you will do those things.** With activities that need to happen repeatedly — phone calls, social media posts, or coffee dates, for example — assign them a frequency or quantity. This could be once per week or ten times per day.

6. **What you did, and what results you achieved.** Be sure to track what actually happened, not just what you planned for. It's the only way you'll know whether your plan is working, and if you're working the plan.

***

If you're already familiar with my *Get Clients Now!* system, you'll recognize these six components. Have you fallen off the gotta-have-a-system wagon? Perhaps it's time to climb back on.

If you're not acquainted with my system yet, I'd love it if you gave it a try. But my real point is that you need *some* system in order for your marketing to succeed.

We entrepreneurs can be an unruly bunch. We often resist systems and structures. After all, many of us went into business to have more independence and control over our destiny. But making use of an effective system can actually be freeing.

"Once I complete the marketing tasks I've chosen," a student told me, "I can stop worrying about marketing and spend the rest of my time as I like. What a relief!"

Why not take a few minutes right now and sketch out the beginnings of your own marketing system? You have very little to lose and much to gain.

START YOUR MARKETING RIGHT
❖

When launching a professional practice or service business, the success of your first few months of operation is crucial. If you are a typical service business owner, you're starting up with less capital than a storefront or product-based business. You are likely to have the expectation that you will begin earning income right away.

You may also have fewer business assets to use as loan collateral than other types of businesses do, and will have to use your personal credit if funds run low.

Here are three important steps to take when launching a new service business that will guarantee your success.

1. Get clients before you start. Find a way to moonlight while maintaining another source of income. Beginning your business with existing clients will give you confidence and start building your referral base. Satisfied customers will provide you with testimonial quotes and a client list for your marketing kit, and references you can give to prospective clients.

Starting up with clients already on the books will hopefully provide you with immediate income. But if you find it difficult to get paying clients at the beginning, volunteer your services for a non-profit organization, or barter with another professional for something you need. You'll still get all the other benefits above.

2. Notify everyone you know. And I do mean everyone. Don't wait until your business is successful to announce it. Go through every address book you have — on your computer, phone, and in your desk drawer. Review the rosters of associations you belong to and from events you've attended. Find your holiday card list. Look through your checkbook and credit card statements for all the people you already do business with. Anyone who might remember you belongs on your announcement list.

Compose an announcement about your new business to send each of these people. This might be a formal announcement card: "Michele Baudouin is pleased to announce the launch of her consulting practice, Strategic Business Solutions, providing strategic planning and productivity consulting to the financial services industry."

> If you find that marketing keeps taking a back seat to other responsibilities, do whatever it takes to shift your priorities.

Or it may be a personal email to each person. It could be a personalized letter sent by mail with a business card enclosed. Don't send any marketing materials at this point, just an announcement.

Send your announcements out in small batches, then — very important! — place a follow-up phone call to each person about a week later. Remind them of your connection, if necessary, and offer to answer their questions about your new business. Ask what they are doing these days, and if there's any way you can help them. Tell them what kind of clients you are looking for, and ask if they would feel comfortable referring potential clients to you.

3. Follow a marketing plan. You'll notice that I'm saying follow a plan, not just write it. That's what most folks do who take the trouble to plan their marketing at all — they write a plan and stick it in a file. You need to build in time and money for regular marketing from the very beginning of your business. Once you get busy with clients, you'll find you have precious little time for it. Regardless of whether you have business or not, never stop marketing.

Be sure what you have is a plan, not just a strategy. Rather than listing ideas on how you might market your business, pick a few activities you will actually be able to do over the next few months. Estimate how much time and money each one will take, and see if that is manageable for you. Then assign dates to each activity that looks doable, and put them in your calendar.

If you find that marketing keeps taking a back seat to other responsibilities, do whatever it takes to shift your priorities. Unless you have a long waiting list of clients eager to work with you, the *only* two activities that should take precedence over marketing are serving your existing clients and getting out the invoices.

WHAT KIND OF MARKETING PLAN DOES A SELF-EMPLOYED PROFESSIONAL NEED?

❖

You need a marketing plan to get clients. That's the first thing to know. A professional who tells you that he or she has gotten plenty of clients without ever having a plan is either:

a) working way too hard,
b) not telling you the truth about how many clients they have,
c) working a plan that they've never written down, or
d) one of those rare, incredibly charismatic individuals who seem to draw an audience as soon as they enter a room.

I find that most of the time, successful professionals who claim to not have a plan fall into the "c" category. They are working from a plan in their head. If you can do that, more power to you. Most people — myself included — need to write a plan down in order to keep it straight.

Now, what kind of plan do you need? Here's the kind you don't need — the sort of marketing plan that a startup business writes to entice potential investors, or the type a corporation uses to guide the activities of its marketing department.

If you Google "marketing plan example," it's those kinds of plans that you'll see. That's what you'll find in most books on writing a marketing plan, too, even those supposedly aimed at small business.

Those big-business-y marketing plans include pages and pages of data, analysis, and speculations... and usually no more than one or two paragraphs about what the business actually plans to do to get customers.

Even then, those paragraphs typically contain nothing but vague statements like "leverage social media and word of mouth" or "explore relationships with local newspapers."

No, what you as a self-employed professional — a microbusiness — need is a marketing action plan. Here's what it should have in it:

1. **Defined goal:** In order to get anywhere, you need to know where you're trying to get. Your marketing plan should begin with a statement of what exactly you'd like to achieve, in immediately measurable terms. For example, "three new full-paying clients," or "one new project with a budget of at least $10,000," or "two new weekly appointments."

> ...successful professionals who claim to not have a plan... are working from a plan in their head. If you can do that, more power to you.

2. **Specific action steps:** Your plan should state exactly what you're going to do, as specifically as possible. Examples: "Make two follow-up calls daily." "Post to my blog once per week." "Contact two new potential referral partners weekly." "Spend 30 minutes posting/sharing/interacting on Facebook each day."

3. **Calendar dates:** A plan with no relationship to the calendar isn't yet a plan. It's just a list of ideas. Your goal should include by when you intend to achieve it. Your action steps need to have an established start and end date. In other words, when will you begin taking the steps you've laid out, and for how long do you plan to take them?

This sort of focused specificity in your plan makes it very powerful. Notice how much more likely it is that you will see results from a plan that says, "attend one live networking event per week," than from one where you have a list of possible marketing approaches that includes simply "networking."

I like the marketing plan that I designed and thousands of self-employed professionals use — *Get Clients Now!* — but you can use any type of marketing plan you like. As long, that is, as you remember to include the three critical elements of a defined goal, specific action steps, and calendar dates when those steps will be taken.

Oh yes, and write it all down.

STOP REACTING AND START PRO-ACTING TO MARKET YOUR BUSINESS

❖

If you're answering calls, replying to emails and posts, responding to invitations, and receiving referrals and leads, it probably feels like you're taking a lot of action to market your business. But it may be that a good deal of what you're engaged in is actually RE-action.

Waiting to hear from the right prospects is nowhere near as productive as proactively taking steps to seek them out. And a stream of incoming communications can take up time and energy, but doesn't always lead to closed sales.

Consider these suggestions for getting out of reaction mode and becoming more proactive in your marketing.

Reactive: Accept referrals and leads as they happen to come to you.
Proactive: Identify likely referral partners and build relationships with them.

Any sort of networking usually produces leads and referrals, but when they're unsuitable, they just take up your time.

An interior designer I know joined a networking group and started receiving referrals from other members. But none of them were appropriate for her high-end business. She not only had to spend time responding to these off-target prospects, she also had to find tactful ways of explaining to her networking buddies that she served only wealthier clients.

Instead of just getting to know more people, make sure they're the right people. Intentionally seek out folks who are in contact with your ideal clients on a regular basis, then let them know how your business can help those clients. Targeted networking will turn into targeted referrals.

Reactive: Accept invitations to networking groups and business meetings as they come to you.

Proactive: Seek out the people, groups, and events most likely to lead to your ideal clients.

> Instead of beginning your day by seeing who has contacted you; start by deciding who you want to contact.

Where you meet people will influence who you have a chance to meet. My interior designer acquaintance joined that networking group just because someone invited her; she knew nothing about it before joining. When it turned out to not be a good fit, she got smart and began looking for better places to network.

By asking others with a high-end clientele about their networking habits, she discovered a leads group of professionals serving wealthy clients. The group included a financial planner, personal banker, insurance broker, estate attorney, real estate agent, residential architect, and a landscaper.

By joining this group, she was in regular contact with people who not only knew clients in the right income bracket, they also were likely to know exactly when the clients might need design help.

Reactive: Respond to the prospects you've met or heard from most recently.

Proactive: Follow up consistently with your best prospects.

Especially when you get busy, it's easy to fall into the habit of doing only what's in front of you. People you just met, and calls or emails you've recently received, can consume all your attention. But what about the prospects you met last month, or who you talked to a couple of weeks ago? Instead of using a "last in; first out" approach, prioritize your follow-up.

A client of mine with an executive coaching practice felt like he was drowning in possibilities. Then he decided to concentrate his follow-up on just five companies who met all his criteria: they needed his services, matched his experience, and could afford to pay. Instead of being pulled in a dozen directions, his focused follow-up quickly led to a contract.

Reactive: Try out the "flavor of the month" as your new marketing approach.

Proactive: Decide on a practical, realistic marketing plan and employ it consistently.

Being overly reactive isn't always about responding to communications. Sometimes it's about responding to ideas. When someone suggests an exciting new way you might get more clients, it's natural to feel drawn to it. But before reacting to suggestions like these, pause and consider whether this new approach will produce better results than what you already have planned.

What will it cost in time and money to change direction? What momentum or opportunities might you lose by not completing what you've begun? What would you have to let go of in order to make good use of a new approach?

If you've already put considerable effort into your existing marketing strategy, why throw it out the window now just because someone suggests another approach "might" be better?

Reactive: Start your day by responding to emails, phone calls, incoming postal mail, and social media posts.

Proactive: Begin each day by working on your own highest priority.

This one change in how you spend your time can make a dramatic difference in the results you're able to produce. Instead of beginning your day by seeing who has contacted you; start by deciding who you want to contact. Tackle your marketing outreach or other important marketing projects first thing in the morning, before checking email, voice mail, Facebook, or Twitter. By making marketing the first thing you do, you'll also make sure it gets done.

Remember, whenever you react to others, you are usually helping them achieve *their* goals. But when you proactively set your own agenda, you are most likely working toward *yours*.

HOW MUCH MARKETING IS JUST ENOUGH?

❖

In my early years as an entrepreneur, a wise mentor taught me about the "just enough" principle. "An entrepreneur's to-do list is endless," she said. "If you ever want to be able to work less than sixty hours a week, you need to figure out how much of anything is just enough."

The one area of entrepreneurship that probably generates the longest to-do list is marketing and sales. When you think of all the ways you could potentially market your business, and compare that to what you are doing now, the implications can be terrifying. Even if you worked 100 hours per week and had a marketing budget equal to last year's total revenue, you could never tackle it all.

But if you can determine how much marketing is just enough to bring in the level of business you want, as well as pay for itself, you can create a functional marketing plan that allows you to sleep at night. The trick is finding that just-enough point.

Right-Sizing Your Sales and Marketing Tactics

Take networking, for example. If you attend three networking events per week, and at each one you make three or four useful contacts, is that enough, too little, or too much? Well, that depends on whether you have enough time to follow up with the people you meet.

If you are able to follow up with each of your new contacts appropriately, a three-times-per-week networking frequency is sustainable. But if you find yourself scrambling to make contact with that many newly-met people before they forget who you are, you're probably attending too many events.

You've exceeded "just enough" and are now wasting your time.

The same principle can be applied to prospecting. At what point do you stop adding new leads to your prospect list, and reaching out to people who don't yet know you, and instead concentrate on closing sales with the folks you already have in the pipeline?

Take a close look at the prospects you already have. Have you followed up with every one of them within the last thirty days? Or if you already know their needs are urgent, within the last ten days? If not, you should probably slow down on collecting new leads and spend more time on follow-up.

> You'll likely discover there is a sweet spot, where the amount of effort you put in correlates to what you get back.

Or, if you're on top of all your follow-up activities, you should back off on following up, and focus on adding new prospects to your list. Either way, you should stop at just enough.

Discovering Your Sweet Spot

What about publishing an ezine, writing a blog, or sending email broadcasts or postal mailings? How often is just enough to publish or mail? The answer will vary depending on your goals. If you are publishing or mailing to increase your credibility or build relationships with your audience, you'll be seeking different results than if you are trying to elicit a direct response measurable by increased sales. But there is always a just-enough point to be found.

With a blog, for example, try this experiment, once you have some regular readers. Write a new post weekly for two weeks, then twice a week for two weeks, then daily for two weeks. Keep track of how much time it takes you, how your readers respond, and what impact it appears to have on your goals. Then go the other direction, and post only twice per week for two weeks, then just weekly for two weeks. What do you notice?

You'll likely discover there is a sweet spot, where the amount of effort you put in correlates to what you get back. Going beyond that point and doing more has little additional impact, but doing less than the required threshold reduces the payoff so much that your efforts seem wasted.

Finding Just Enough

No matter what marketing or sales approach you choose, the secret to finding the just-enough point is to start looking for it. Instead of blindly trying to do everything, or blithely ignoring what you don't seem to have time for, become rigorous about comparing what you are doing to the results you are seeing.

Determining how much marketing is just enough may turn out to finally be the answer to finding just enough clients.

THE WORLD'S SIMPLEST MARKETING PLAN
❖

A client once told me she was a "marketing idiot." What she really needed, she said, was the "world's simplest marketing plan." So, we set out to create one for her. Here's what it looked like:

1. Make a list of everyone you know.
2. Tell those people about your business.
3. Ask if they'd like to find out more about it.
4. Tell the interested people more.
5. When you get to the end of the list, contact everyone again.
6. With anyone who fits your client profile, ask if they'd like to work with you.
7. With anyone who doesn't fit, tell them what the profile is, and ask if they know anyone who fits.
8. Add any new people to your list and repeat steps 2-4.
9. When you get to the end of the list, contact everyone again. Update them on your latest work or provide them with useful information.
10. With anyone who fits your client profile, ask if they are ready to work with you yet.
11. With anyone who doesn't fit, remind them what the client profile is, and ask if they know anyone *else* who knows people that fit.
12. Add any new people to your list and repeat steps 2-8.

We never got any further than step 12 in her plan, because by the time she got there, several things had happened:
- With a plan in front of her, she knew what to do, so she set aside time for it, and took action.

- Because she was taking consistent action, she was also following up with her contacts on a regular basis.
- By telling another person about her plan (me, in this case), she created accountability for herself.
- Because she was setting aside marketing time regularly, following up with contacts consistently, and reinforcing her commitments with outside accountability, she began to produce results. *Enough* results — in the form of new clients — that

> With a plan in front of her, she knew what to do, so she set aside time for it, and took action.

we never needed to continue her plan to step 13.

If you're skeptical that a marketing plan as simple as this one might work for you, consider the following:
- You may be able to add to the list of "everyone you know" from more sources than you think. Consider your former co-workers, people you went to school with, members of your professional associations, people in your social media networks, neighbors near your office or home, members of clubs and activity groups you belong to, relatives, and personal friends.
- As your list grows, you can refine it by eliminating people who are neither appropriate prospects nor likely referral sources. Just don't do this too soon, as some of your contacts may surprise you with their interest.
- Telling people about your business and asking them questions can take many different forms. You can call them, email them, write them a letter, send them a postcard, or interact with them on social media.

- Updating contacts about your latest work or providing them with useful information can take many different forms also. You can call them, email them a note, mail them a newsletter or postcard, put them on your ezine list (if they've agreed to subscribe), share a social media update with them, or let them know about an article, case study, blog post, podcast, video, or event.

As you can see, a simple marketing plan can become quite sophisticated, especially over time. You can begin with phone calls and emails to your inner circle, then both expand your list to include more people, and expand your range of tools for contacting and updating them.

Why not give this simple marketing plan a try? Adapt it to the size of your contact list and the tools you already have. Make sure you follow all the steps faithfully. For example, don't leave out the step where you "ask if they'd like to work with you."

Be sure also to set aside time to work your plan, and create some accountability for yourself. Share your plan with a friend, colleague, coach, or action group, success team, support group, or mastermind group.

As you have time, resources, and the need, add new tools for contacting and updating your contacts, such as a newsletter, blog, podcasts, videos, events, or social media channels. Just don't let the time and effort it takes to create those tools detract from faithfully working your plan with the tools you already have.

You may just find, like my client did, that this simple marketing plan is the only one you'll ever need.

IF YOUR MARKETING WORKS,
ARE YOU PREPARED TO SELL?
❖

Most of the available information and real-world effort aimed at getting more clients focuses on promotion and attraction. You'll find plenty of advice on how to tell the world about your business, make the phone ring, or get inquiries to arrive in your email inbox.

But once you've been marketing yourself for a while, you discover that turning those prospects into paying clients can be pretty darned difficult. I find that many professionals are simply not prepared to sell to the prospects they attract.

When you're selling a professional service, marketing doesn't end at a sale; it ends in a sales conversation.

People don't buy accounting or coaching or graphic design or management consulting as the result of seeing your ad, getting your letter, or visiting your website. They make their decision to hire you as the result of a conversation where you find out what they need, tell them what you have to offer, and the two of you see if there's a match. That's selling.

If you put all your effort into marketing, then aren't prepared to sell when a prospective client gets in touch, you'll waste good prospects and the work you did to get them to contact you. Here's what you need to be ready to sell.

1. Get your basics together. An essential element for successful selling is a clear, concise description of what you do, with an emphasis on the benefits of working with you and the results you can produce. This is not the same thing as simply citing your education and experience. Prospects don't want to hear what you might be capable of; they want to know how you can solve the problem they have today.

Be prepared to discuss your rates. While you may need detailed information to quote a firm price, don't stall prospects with a vague "we'll need to talk about that" when they ask what you charge. Whether you work by the hour, day, month, or project, you can answer with a range of prices or examples of what you've charged in the past.

Prospects don't want to waste time in conversation if your services cost far more than their budget will allow, and neither do you.

> Developing… steps and tools for effective selling will make it possible to convert more of your prospects into clients.

2. Be prepared with qualifying questions. Not everyone who contacts you will be a real prospect. You'll need to ask questions to *select in* the prospects you want and *select out* the ones you don't. What problem do they need to solve? How important is it to them? What made them contact you vs. a competitor? How much are they expecting to pay? How soon will they be making a decision?

Their answers will reveal how appropriate they are to become your clients, and their readiness and willingness to hire you.

3. Determine what you want prospects to do. What do you want your prospects to do when they first contact you? Schedule an appointment for an in-person presentation? Provide details so you can make a quote or proposal? Review your offerings to choose appropriate options? Come in for an evaluation? Sign up for a sample session or introductory seminar?

Whatever you determine this first step is, your entire response to their query should be focused on getting them to take it. Lead them through your sales process; don't make them figure it out.

4. Be ready to follow up. Most initial conversations end with a next step rather than a closed sale. Gain your prospects' agreement to this step, and follow-up will be much easier.

When they agree to schedule a presentation, evaluation, sample session, or introductory seminar, confirm the date on the spot and follow up with a reminder. When they agree to send their details for a quote or to make selections from your offerings, tell them how to do it and follow up with a form, list of questions, or link.

When it becomes clear your prospects aren't ready to commit to a purchase, you'll need to follow up as well. Capture all the details you'll need for follow up in your first exchange with them, and ask their permission to do so.

For example, "May I call you next month?' or "May I subscribe you to my newsletter/blog?" or "May I add you to my mailing list for future events or new offerings?" Be prepared to follow up repeatedly until they're ready to act.

5. Have tools to support your strategy. Each one of the steps above requires tools to perform it well. Every professional needs a clear description of services, fee schedule, and list of qualifying questions. Depending on your business, you may also need a presentation, sample session, or intro seminar outline, a quote or request-for-proposal form, and/or online portfolio or catalog.

For follow-up, you need some sort of contact management and calendaring system, and you may also need an email list management system.

Developing these steps and tools for effective selling will make it possible to convert more of your prospects into clients. An organized, well-considered sales process like this will also make you a more confident salesperson.

So — be prepared for your marketing to work by being ready to sell once it does!

THE FIVE "P"S OF PROFESSIONAL SERVICES MARKETING

❖

In 1960, E. Jerome McCarthy introduced the Four "P"s of Marketing as a way to describe the mix of factors required to successfully market a product. McCarthy labeled the Four "P"s as Product, Price, Place (distribution), and Promotion. The idea was that if you could identify the right combination of these elements, your marketing would succeed.

Since then, many have proposed that there are really Five "P"s, suggesting Positioning, Packaging, or People as additions to the mix.

For professionals, consultants, coaches, and freelancers marketing their own services, I don't find that the classic Four "P"s provide much guidance in making the right choices about marketing. Here is a different sort of 5 P's for the typical self-employed professional, who is both the product and the one marketing it at the same time.

1. People: In order to market effectively, people are an essential part of the equation. Some marketing experts have suggested that the "people" component represents the people who deliver the service you are marketing — a critical factor for a service business.

But I think there are two other types of people important to your marketing: the people you are marketing to, and the people who help you spread the word about your business.

To make realistic decisions about marketing, you need to have a clear definition of your target market and understand their needs. Only then can you know who you should be delivering your marketing messages to, and what you need to communicate. With a solid definition of your target market and a well-defined message in hand, you can reach out directly to the people who might become your clients, and ask other people to pass your message along to those they know.

2. Positioning: Your marketplace is crowded with competitors, and your prospects are besieged with marketing messages. For your message to find its way through all this noise, it must be exactly on target. In any professional field, it's not enough to simply describe what you do. You must be able to tell your prospects exactly how your work helps them solve problems and reach goals, and the benefits and results they can expect to see from it.

> In the classic marketing formula, the emphasis was on promotion... But that's only one piece of the puzzle. You also need to include attraction...

What this targeted messaging requires is that you become very specific about not only who your offer is for, but what it will help them do, and why your solution is the right one for them. You must position your business in the mind of your prospective clients as the best possible choice for exactly what they need.

Broadcasting a muddy or generic marketing message won't be enough. Your clients need to understand "what's in it for me?"

3. Personal credibility: A professional service isn't like a pie or a pair of shoes. It can't be tasted or tried on before the customer decides to buy. Clients are wary — and justifiably so — of committing to spend hundreds or thousands of dollars on something they haven't been able to experience in advance. Without tangible evidence to go by, they base their decision on how much they trust you. A significant portion of your marketing activities should be aimed at increasing your personal credibility.

Writing articles, blogging, giving talks, media interviews, and volunteering in your professional association or community will all contribute to your credibility. But one of the best ways to build trust is also the simplest. Allow clients to get to know you better before pushing for a sale.

Casual conversations by phone, email, or social media; having lunch or coffee; meeting at business or social events; and connecting at networking meetings will contribute to the know-like-and-trust factor that makes people buy.

4. Push plus pull: In the classic marketing formula, the emphasis was on promotion — pushing your message out to the world at large. But that's only one piece of the puzzle. You also need to include attraction — pulling toward you exactly those clients you want.

For a self-employed professional, push-style marketing includes cold calling, unsolicited mail or email, promotional social media posts, paid advertising (online and off), promotional events like trade shows, and some forms of PR, like blasting out press releases.

Pull marketing, on the other hand, is focused on building affinity and connections. To attract clients in your niche, you might develop referral partnerships, become visible at networking events, network with prospects and colleagues online, get booked as a public speaker, have your articles and blog posts published, land media interviews, or build a content-rich website.

You'll find it much easier to make a sale when clients contact you as the result of hearing about you from someone else, or after sampling your expertise for free.

5. Persistence: The final element every professional needs in his or her marketing mix is persistence. Without this component, your best intentions with the other four will fail.

You have to connect with people over and over again before they will remember your message. Your positioning will only be established when prospects hear about you more than once. Building your personal credibility depends on different types of exposure over a period of time. And both push marketing and pull marketing require repeat contacts in order to pay off.

Try putting these Five "P"s together into a personal marketing mix of your own. As a self-employed professional, I think you'll find them much more pertinent than the classic Four.

HOW TO AVOID THE FEAST OR FAMINE TRAP

❖

It often seems that it's the destiny of the self-employed professional to exist in a constant state of feast or famine. Either you are working day and night to keep up with client demands, or you're wondering how much is left in your savings account and whether the phone will ever ring again.

When you're having a feast of business, there's plenty of money coming in, you're getting recognition for your talents, and your energy level is usually high. But you may also feel constantly pressed for time, have to disappoint some clients you can't adequately serve, and lose out on future business because you can't respond to new opportunities.

When a business famine strikes, you have the time to develop new business and provide good service to the clients you still have. But you may also be low on cash and not feeling so good about yourself, which gets in the way of effective marketing.

There's a simple answer to this dilemma. You need to market for new clients consistently and persistently, no matter what state your business is currently in. But like many simple answers, this one is not necessarily easy.

Here are some suggestions for how to always make time for marketing.

1. Sometimes the customer comes second. If you spend all your time doing client work, you will go out of business. You need to set aside time not only for marketing, but to answer mail, keep up in your field, and oh yes, collect what you are owed. Every time you rush to help a client with what they call an emergency, you set a precedent that you will be available on short notice. Learn to say no compassionately, but firmly, when constant client requests interfere with you running your business to your own benefit.

2. Establish a time budget for marketing. It's helpful to have two different time budgets — one for when you are busy, and one for when things are slow. If you're busy, a minimal budget will keep your marketing rolling.

In two hours per week, you can have coffee with a prospect, make phone calls, send out emails, connect on social media, or make contacts about speaking. When business is slow, you should increase your time budget up to 30-50% of your work week — more, if you aren't doing any client work at all.

> Sometimes the customer comes second. If you spend all your time doing client work, you will go out of business.

3. Make marketing a priority in your calendar. Work expands to fill the time allotted to it. Think of the last time you wrote a proposal or page of web copy. If the deadline was a week away, you may have written and re-written until it was perfect. If the deadline was the same day, you probably miraculously completed it on time.

When you block out marketing time in your calendar, and schedule other important activities around it, you will find that those other activities somehow get done. Treat your marketing time just like an appointment. If something truly urgent comes up, reschedule it; don't just erase it.

4. Get your marketing done first. Sit down at your desk in the morning, and before listening to voice mail, reading email, hopping on social media, or looking at your client projects, tackle whatever marketing activities are on your agenda for the day. Spend 15 minutes, an hour, or two hours — whatever makes sense for your current marketing time budget — and then start your regular day. This has the added benefit of allowing you to engage in marketing when you are fresh.

If despite your best efforts, you do hit a famine period, there are some things you can do.

1. Take advantage of the lull to make a plan. This could be a new marketing plan, or it could be a business plan where you do some financial modeling or revisit your strategic direction. I usually do this myself during the month of December, when I can expect a seasonal slowdown as my regular clients take vacation time and new clients don't want to begin until January.

2. Send out a reminder. This could be in the form of a postcard, email broadcast, or social media posts, with an announcement, special offer, or helpful information for your target market. If you are thinking, "Send a reminder to who?" you need to take some to time to update and…

3. Use your contact management system. Every independent professional needs some type of contact management system (CMS) to track your clients and prospects, whether it's sheets of paper in a three-ring binder, software on your computer, or an app in the cloud.

When business is slow, every potential client in your CMS who hasn't heard from you in the last thirty days is worth contacting. You are much more likely to get a client quickly from follow up than you are from contacting someone new.

If you use a CMS, you'll be able to…

4. Research where your business comes from. If you track the source of every lead, you can then determine which sources delivered people who became clients, then how much money each of those clients spent with you. It's an extremely worthwhile use of some down time to find out which sources of business put the most money in your pocket, and then see what you can do to replicate them.

If you do a good job at consistent and persistent marketing, inevitably you will attract more business than you can handle, at least at certain times. Don't be so afraid of this possibility that you allow it to hold back your marketing! If you're not available, many clients will wait for you. Having a waiting list makes you more desirable, and it also allows you to raise your rates because of the perceived demand for your services.

Don't stay trapped in the feast or famine cycle. A steady diet of just enough clients will feed a happier, healthier, wealthier you.

IS IT A GREAT OPPORTUNITY
OR A WASTE OF TIME?

❖

As business owners, we are frequently offered "opportunities" that may deliver a significant return, but also have the potential to take up a great deal of time. You may be asked to provide your expertise, collaborate on a project, help organize an event, or partner on a new venture. How do you decide which of these offers to accept, and which to decline?

The first thing to do is determine exactly what kind of opportunity you are being offered. Here are the five types of opportunities that business owners typically encounter, and some suggested questions to ask yourself about each.

1. Paying business with an immediate return. The project you are being asked to work on has already been funded and you will be paid for your contribution. If you are being offered your standard rate, and you have the time available, you will almost always say yes to these opportunities.

But, if the price offered is less than you could get elsewhere, ask yourself what would make accepting a lower price worthwhile. How likely is it that you will get that something else from this project?

2. Business with a possible future return. The project or venture does not yet have the funding to pay you. You are being asked to make your contribution in return for compensation at some future date. On a project like this, there is no guarantee you will ever be paid, no matter how good the promises sound. How much is at stake? Can you afford that much risk?

3. Unpaid work that may lead to paying work. You are being asked to contribute in return for market visibility, professional credibility, or community goodwill. How much of those benefits would make your contribution worthwhile? Are you likely to get that much? Would you be more likely to get what you need by contributing elsewhere?

4. Contributing to a good cause. You are being asked to donate your time, goods, or resources to support an organization, person, or cause. There may be no tangible return of any kind, or you may receive some public recognition. Is this an entity you enthusiastically support? Are you eager to help this entity regardless of whether you get anything back? Will knowing that you've done something to help be enough to make it worthwhile?

> Are all your existing obligations adequately handled? If you are already struggling to meet deadlines, it's probably not the time to take on something new.

5. Having fun. Compensation or reward isn't an issue here, but your personal fulfillment is. Is this an activity you truly enjoy? Are those who will accompany you people who you like to spend time with? Would you have chosen to do it if you hadn't been asked? With the limited time you may have available for fun, is this the way you would most like to use it?

It's difficult for many people to say no to new opportunities, particularly when a friend is asking. Years ago, professional organizers Pam Austin and Celeste Lane shared with me some of the tools they use to help clients manage their time and priorities as well as filing systems and paper flow. One of these was a checklist titled "Before You Say Yes," which appears in a modified form below:

- Are all your existing obligations adequately handled? If you are already struggling to meet deadlines, it's probably not the time to take on something new.
- What will this new opportunity cost you in time, money, energy, emotion, or stress? Do you have all that available to expend?
- Do you want to do this 100%? It's normal to feel some fear or nervousness about doing something new, but put any fear aside for the moment and check in with your desire level.
- Is the person asking you a stranger? If so, have you checked him or her out? Celeste suggests you meet with someone new at least three times, and check some references, before you make a commitment.
- Is there another way? Would there be an easier or cheaper path that would bring you the same result?

Whenever someone asks you to be part of something other than paying business at your usual rate, take the time to go through the above checklist. And memorize this phrase to use: "I'll think about it and get back to you."

MARKETING OR SELLING:
WHICH IS MORE IMPORTANT?

❖

A question I often get from clients and students goes something like this: "I've been collecting marketing ideas... and I have a drawer full! I also have a stack of promising leads I've accumulated. And I know it's important to stay visible, so I keep marketing, but then I just end up with more names in the stack. How do I prioritize all this?"

If you've ever wondered something similar, you may have lost sight of a very important truth — the way to win the business game is not to collect the most leads; it's to make the most sales. Marketing activities that increase your number of sales are good, and activities that don't are bad, even if they bring in plenty of leads. If you don't follow up on the leads your marketing produces, you are throwing away your time and money.

The main purpose of marketing strategies like posting on social media, public speaking, blogging, writing articles, promotional events, and advertising is to gain visibility and acquire leads. (A secondary purpose of the first four strategies can be to gain credibility.) Why do you want to be more visible? It's not just so people will know who you are and what you do, it's so they will do business with you.

If someone has already expressed interest in doing business with you, contact them. Do it now. Memorize this rule — following up on hot, or even warm, client leads is always more important than marketing for more visibility.

There is a simple diagnostic test you can take to see where you need to focus your marketing vs. selling efforts — the Universal Marketing Cycle. Think of the marketing and sales process as a water system that begins by filling your pipeline with contacts. The pipeline empties into your follow-up pool, which you are continually dipping into.

Your intent is to move the leads further along in the system, to having a sales conversation and finally closing the sale.

Where are you stuck in this sequence? Is it in filling the pipeline to begin with? Or is the pipeline full, but you haven't been following up? Perhaps you have been following up, but don't seem to be getting to the conversation stage. Or maybe you are having conversations but

> ...the way to win the business game is not to collect the most leads; it's to make the most sales.

not closing sales. Wherever you seem to be stuck is the area that needs more effort.

When you have promising leads you aren't contacting, the follow-up stage is clearly your stuck place. Take that stack of leads and sort them into three categories: prospective clients, useful networking contacts, and other. Now sort the prospective clients into hot, warm, and cold. Stop right there and follow up with all the hot and warm leads.

If — and I do mean if — you still need to do more work about marketing after following up with all those leads, go to the networking contacts and sort them into two groups: people who can lead you directly to prospective clients, and people who can lead you to other marketing opportunities, e.g., a new networking group or a speaking engagement. Stop, and — you guessed it — follow up with the people who might have leads for you.

You should now have three groups left: cold client leads, people who can lead you to marketing opportunities, and other. Now is the time to decide whether you need to do something new to market yourself at all. Look at what you have been doing so far to get all those hot and warm leads you had. Maybe you just need to do more of the same.

If that's true, put those cold leads aside, because you'll have more hot and warm ones shortly. If you need to do something different to get better leads than what you had, go ahead and explore one of the new marketing possibilities in your second group, or one of the ideas stashed away in that drawer. And that "other" group of leads? Throw them away. They are just cluttering up your marketing pipeline.

NOT ENOUGH CLIENTS?
WHAT'S IN YOUR WAY?
❖

What's stopping you from getting all the clients you want? Do you know? The answer to this one question may be the key to making your marketing more successful.

It would seem from the questions people ask me about marketing that everyone is trying to fix just one type of problem — how to fill their marketing pipeline with more new prospects.

"What else should I be doing to attract potential clients?" they ask. "Where else can I go to find people who might hire me?" or "How can I be more visible online so people will contact me?" or "Should I be finding prospects by cold calling, using Twitter, running ads, giving talks, writing articles…?"

All their questions — and it seems all their efforts — are aimed at finding ways to make contact with new people who might become clients. And every time they identify another activity that might help their pipeline get fuller, they want to add it to their ever-growing to-do list.

But is this really what's stopping them from getting more clients? Is this what's stopping you? If you are already marketing yourself in four or five different ways, will increasing that to seven or eight different ways produce better results? Or alternatively, if you drop everything you're doing now, and start using four or five brand new marketing approaches, will that do the trick?

In my experience, it probably won't. Continuing to try new and different approaches to fill your marketing pipeline will more often result in overwhelm, wasted effort, and failure than it will in new clients.

Instead of trying to fix your marketing by just seeking out more ways to meet people or collect names, email addresses and phone numbers, stop for a moment. What is the problem you're trying to solve? In other words, what's really getting in the way of your marketing success?

Listed below are the five most common marketing problems, and questions to ask yourself to see which ones might be yours. They're presented in order of priority -- problem #1 needs to be fixed before tackling problem #2, and so on. Consider whether making changes in one of these areas might be exactly the fix your marketing needs.

> Finding new or different marketing approaches -- the place where most people start to fix their marketing -- is actually the last area to consider.

1. Hands-on time: Are you spending enough time proactively marketing? Not just getting ready to market, or thinking about how to market, or feeling resistant to marketing, but truly taking steps that will lead directly to landing clients?

If you're not spending enough time marketing your business, fixing other problem areas won't help much. Start keeping track of how much time you spend actively marketing each week. Most independent professionals find they need to spend from four to sixteen hours weekly -- less when you're busy with paying work; more when you're not.

2. Target market: Do you have a clearly defined target market which you can describe in five words or less? Does this market already know they need your services? And are you spending most of your time marketing to exactly that group?

Once you feel confident you are dedicating enough time to marketing, the next hurdle is making sure you're marketing to the right people. Focusing your efforts on a specific target group with a defined need for your services will make everything you do more effective.

3. Marketing message: Do your descriptions of your services name the benefits you offer and results you produce for your target market? And are these benefits and results that this market is looking for? Do you deliver your message every time you make contact?

Letting prospective clients know exactly how you can help them will make the most of the time you spend marketing to a defined audience. Your message needs to be clear, focused on the client's needs, and typically delivered multiple times to the same prospects.

4. Follow-through: Do you have a system for following up with every prospect until they say either yes or no? Are you able to complete all the steps for each marketing approach you are using to make it pay off?

Without follow-through, much of your marketing effort is wasted. The typical prospect will need to hear from you (or about you) five to seven times before deciding to work with you. And most marketing approaches need a follow-through element to succeed. For example, attending networking events requires post-event follow-up with the people you meet. Social media requires regular participation, not just posting when you have something to promote.

5. Marketing approach: Are the strategies and tactics you are using to reach your market the most effective approaches available to you? Are they appropriate for your target market, and a good match for your skills and personality?

Only after addressing the first four problem areas above should you think about changing how you market. Because in truth, your tactics may not need to change. Whether you've been marketing yourself with cold calling, public speaking, or social media, once you are spending enough time, marketing to the right people, delivering a targeted message, and following through on all your efforts, your results will improve dramatically.

Finding new or different marketing approaches –- the place where most people start to fix their marketing -– is actually the last area to consider. The most effective approaches are those that include personal contact with your prospects, increase your credibility, and lend themselves to building relationships over time. And, approaches that match your skills and personality are more likely to succeed because you will use them instead of resisting them.

Once you know what might be stopping your marketing from being successful, make a commitment to fix what's really wrong. Resist the temptation (and hype) to keep trying new "silver bullet" marketing tactics or overloading yourself with endless possibilities. Finding the right answers will be much easier when you're trying to solve the right problem.

MORE IS NOT NECESSARILY BETTER

Have you ever noticed what happens when a self-employed professional speaks up in a group or makes a post online saying, "I'm not getting enough clients. What should I do?"

Inevitably, everyone responds with a different marketing idea: "Have you tried joining a leads group?" "Running an AdWords campaign really worked for me." "You should consider starting a podcast." "You need a Facebook page." "What about writing a blog?"

And so, the client-deficient professional walks away with a long list of new marketing ideas to try. You would think our professional would now feel empowered and hopeful about the likelihood of getting more clients. But in reality, a more common reaction to a deluge of supposedly helpful suggestions is to feel confused and overwhelmed.

How do you know which of those ideas will pay off for you? Should you be doing all of these things? If not, which ones should you try first? Where do you find out how to do something you know nothing about, like joining a leads group or starting a podcast? Shouldn't you be finishing your website first? And what about those follow-up calls you've been meaning to make? Yikes!

The Slippery Slope of "More" Marketing

It's human nature to offer as much advice as possible to someone with a problem. It's also human nature to always look for a better mousetrap than the one you already have. But the combination of these two human proclivities can have a deadly result for professionals seeking clients.

Let's say you are just starting out in business, and you have attended a few networking events, started a simple website, and mailed out a few letters to prospective clients, all with minimal results so far. You wonder, quite naturally, if you are doing the right things. So, you ask for some advice.

Your peers, wanting to be helpful, make many different suggestions about what you should do. You, wanting to find the best possible mousetrap, decide to try them all at least once. In addition to what you are already doing, you are going to join a leads group, launch an AdWords campaign, start a podcast, launch a Facebook page, and create a blog.

> When you're in a restaurant and the dessert menu arrives... do you order five different kinds and try a sample of each one?

You attend the leads group twice, then find you are too busy on other marketing tasks to make the meetings. Your AdWords campaign is getting plenty of clicks and costing you a bundle, but no clients are resulting from it, probably because you never finished updating the copy on your website.

You take a class to learn how to start a podcast, but get bogged down in the technical details. You launch a Facebook page, but your only likes are from your family and personal friends. You post to the blog a few times, but never get around to doing anything to promote it.

Meanwhile, you haven't had a chance to follow up on the contacts you made at networking events before you got all this new advice, nor have you ever called any of the people you sent marketing letters to.

And with all this effort, you still aren't getting enough clients. Not that you would have any time to serve more clients anyway, because you are too busy marketing!

How to Do Better with Less

This is the unhappy, but all too common result of piling idea after idea onto your marketing plate. Lacking the time and resources to execute any of the ideas well, you get poor results. Thinking your original ideas must be wrong, you add even more ideas to the mix. But more is not necessarily better.

When you're in a restaurant and the dessert menu arrives, how often do you order five different kinds and try a sample of each one? Instead, it's much more likely that you consider the menu carefully, weigh your choices, and pick just one dessert for today's meal. You know you can't (or shouldn't) eat five of them, nor do you want to spend your money on ordering five and only taking a bite of each one.

No, you choose one dessert, and most likely, savor it to the last bite. You enjoy it, finish it, and feel satisfied with your meal.

If you applied this same sort of thinking to your marketing, it might work like this. Looking at the menu of possible marketing ideas, you first decide how many ideas you have room for — one, two, three? Then you choose one, two, or three from the menu that best fit your needs and desires.

What do you like doing? What seems like it would be most effective with your target market? What do you already know how to do? What do you have the time and money to do well?

Once you have chosen your ideas, make a commitment to follow them through to completion before you try any others. Finish your dessert before starting the next meal.

Our overwhelmed professional above had already chosen three marketing ideas before getting all that new advice. He/she was attending networking events, working on a website, and mailing letters to prospective clients. It's entirely possible that the only reason those ideas hadn't produced any results yet was because they hadn't been completed.

When you attend a networking event, make time to follow up afterward with the people you meet. Instead of always finding new events to attend, go back to the same ones over and over to build relationships. When you launch a website, get it ready for prime time before you start working on attracting traffic to it. When you mail letters to prospective clients, plan to follow them up with phone calls, and to mail and call again if you don't get a response.

More is not necessarily better. Three simple marketing ideas, executed well, and followed through to completion, may be all you need to build your business. Twenty fancy marketing ideas, executed poorly, and left incomplete due to lack of time and resources, might just drive you out of business instead.

NEW YEAR'S REVOLUTION

❖

No, that's not a typo in the title. Resolutions are easy; most of us make them at least once a year. A revolution, on the other hand, is something you may not have made since you started your business.

Launching a new business is actually quite revolutionary. When you began yours, there were probably many details of your life that changed. Some of those changes were intentional, others accidental; some you liked, some you didn't. Other changes that you always meant to make just never seemed to happen.

Is your business everything you meant it to be? Is it giving you all that you wanted? Are you satisfied, even delighted with how your life as a business owner is turning out? If not, perhaps it's time to start a revolution. Here are some revolutionary ideas you might consider adopting.

1. Serve only those clients you care about and enjoy being with. When you work with people you don't enjoy, everything becomes a struggle. Your clients are an essential part of your business. You wouldn't hire someone you didn't enjoy working with, so why let people you don't like very much hire you?

Begin today to let go of clients you find difficult to work with, and start seeking out the type of client you really had in mind when you started this business. Have the courage to refuse new clients that don't fit your picture of who you most want your business to serve.

2. Make a plan to reach your income goals. Unless you are independently wealthy, your business not only needs to support you, it needs to provide for your future. Setting goals for your desired income level is a good first step, but to reach those goals, you need a plan.

Create a realistic financial model for your business. How many clients, accounts, appointments, billable hours, or contracts will it take to generate the income you want? How much of your time will be required to do that amount of work and also do the marketing required to get it? How much money will it cost you in overhead, marketing costs, and admin help? Put all these elements together to create a model that will produce the results you desire.

> If you're not enjoying the work you do, there's no one to blame but yourself. After all, you're the owner...

3. Take enough time for yourself and those you love. The number one reason entrepreneurs name for going into business is time — more to spend with their families, more flexibility in their work hours, or simply more control over how their time is spent. But how many business owners get this result?

Most self-employed professionals spend either too much time struggling to get clients and earning too little money, or become victims of their own success, working too many hours to fulfill clients' demands. You can overcome these problems by combining the financial modeling described above with the approach to marketing outlined below. And don't forget, if you earn enough, you can hire all the help you need to take more time off.

4. Do more of the work you like doing and less of what you don't. If you're not enjoying the work you do, there's no one to blame but yourself. After all, you're the owner of this enterprise. If you could do a more enjoyable kind of work in the same business you're already in, start now to make the shift. Loyal customers will follow you if you're still offering services they need.

If doing more rewarding work would require an entirely new business, join the ranks of the serial entrepreneurs. You started and ran one business, why not another? Life is much too short to do work you don't enjoy, and it doesn't make much sense if you're working for yourself!

5. Build a marketing system that really works. The definition of a system is "a selection of related components arranged in a specific order to achieve a common end." Does this describe your marketing? Or is it more like a hodgepodge of random elements jumbled together without a clear goal?

To produce better clients, more money, more time for yourself, and more enjoyable work, an effective marketing system may be the universal solution. Don't know how to build one? Start now to learn. Already know how but haven't built it? Get support from a colleague, mentor, coach, or group to make it happen. Have a system but aren't using it? Pull your plan out of the drawer and put it into action.

If you're feeling oppressed by your own business, revolt! Make this the year you take control of your clients, your income, your time, and your marketing. A revolution just may be what it takes to create the business you always dreamed of.

WHAT ARE YOU DOING RIGHT?

❖

What's wrong with my marketing?" That's a question I often hear from clients, students, and readers. It's a useful query, as there frequently are areas where you could do better at marketing and sales. But while the question "what's wrong" can uncover your marketing problems, it doesn't always suggest answers. You may need to ask what you're doing right.

Examining what's already working about your marketing and sales activities can give you valuable clues to how you can improve. Here are some helpful questions to ask yourself, and what they might tell you about where your marketing efforts will produce the best results.

1. Where did your last few clients come from? Consider the new clients you've landed over the past year. Were they referred to you? Did they contact you through your website? Had they heard you speak? Did you cold call them?

Examine the source of all your recent sales and determine exactly how you first came in contact, and what sequence of events led to closing those sales. If you notice a pattern, see how you might repeat your success.

One of my coaching clients, a graphic designer, was spending a considerable amount of her marketing time on approaching ad agencies and corporate marketing departments, with lukewarm results. She told me these had always been her best source of clients in the past, but I asked her to look at where her clients had been coming from lately.

She was surprised to discover that all her recent clients had been referrals from colleagues, such as a copywriter, a photographer, and an art director. When she switched the emphasis of her marketing away from knocking on the doors of large firms, and instead began networking with professionals in related fields, she began seeing better results almost immediately.

2. How have you gotten your best clients? Some clients give us repeat business, pay our fees without quibbling, and are easy to work with, while others want us to work at discount prices and jump through hoops to get and keep their business. Consider who your best clients have been over time, and what you did to find them. Are these approaches you can use again?

> ...when you're self-employed, nobody is going to make you market yourself. Your marketing plan needs to consist of activities you are willing to do.

A marketing communications consultant in one of my classes was struggling with a demanding large client who paid below market rates. She had other, smaller clients who paid better and were much easier to work with. She realized that these small, well-paying clients were all people she had met through a trade association, while the demanding client was someone she had cold-called. Clearly, she needed to stop cold calling and step up participation in the trade group.

3. Where do you get the strongest response from your marketing messages? In what environments do you find that people really connect with what you have to say? Where does it seem like "your people" are, or under what circumstances do you seem to attract potential clients without even trying? This can be a useful query to guide your marketing even if you're new and haven't made many sales yet.

One of my colleagues, a new business coach, was unsure whether to focus on small business owners or corporate executives as his target market, so he was approaching both. But he noticed that entrepreneurs seemed much more interested in talking to him than executives did, and quickly acquired several likely prospects who were all small business owners. He concluded that he could stop searching for his target market, because it seemed to have found him on its own.

4. What marketing activities feel most comfortable and natural to you? Let's face it; when you're self-employed, nobody is going to make you market yourself. Your marketing plan needs to consist of activities you are willing to do. Instead of beating yourself up for what you're not doing, notice what marketing tactics you find to be easier and more attractive.

A change management consultant I was advising felt like a failure at marketing because he avoided attending networking events or calling strangers on the phone. But he realized he was quite comfortable with two types of marketing: writing articles, and having conversations with people he already knew. When he created a marketing plan centered around article writing and building one-to-one relationships, he was at last able to sell himself with ease.

No matter what is wrong with your marketing, there's always a better way to go about it. Looking at what's not working can only take you so far. Then it's time to ask yourself what you're already doing right.

IS IT TIME TO RESET YOUR MARKETING PLAN?

❖

Is your marketing plan producing the results you need? When was the last time you evaluated your plan to see if it is leading you toward success? Are you even using a marketing plan at all? Here are four questions to help you determine whether it's time to reset your plan.

1. Are you getting in touch every month with at least three times as many new clients as you need? Not every prospective client will say yes. You need to have a marketing pipeline filled with prospects, contacts, leads, and referrals that you can draw from. If your marketing activities aren't connecting you each month with three or more times as many prospects as you want in clients, your pipeline won't be full enough to support you.

2. When you sit down to work on marketing, do you know what to do next? Many self-employed professionals find themselves spending more time thinking about how to market than actually doing it. Or simply reacting to outside influences (event invitations, ad solicitations, etc.), rather than proactively choosing what to do.

3. Are you spending the majority of your marketing time using the most effective approaches to get clients? For self-employed professionals, the best ways to get clients all involve building personal connections and establishing your expertise. Posting promos for your business on social media, running ads, or sending promotional email blasts are examples of activities that don't accomplish this.

4. Do you feel excited and motivated about marketing your business? There's no boss looking over your shoulder making you spend time on marketing. When you don't feel engaged and positive about your own marketing, you're more likely to neglect it than to embrace it.

If you didn't answer yes to all of these questions, it's time you had a marketing plan that truly serves you, instead of one that takes up time and money without producing results. Here are some steps to start building a powerful, focused, compelling plan:

> Saying you will "network" is not a plan. Writing that you will "attend one live networking event per week," then putting those dates on your calendar — that's a plan...

- **Identify the two or three marketing strategies most likely to be effective** with your target audience, and spend most of your marketing time using just those strategies. Focus on strategies that help you build connections and position yourself as an expert.

- **For each marketing strategy you plan to use, choose the tactics you feel most comfortable with employing.** If you plan to reach out to prospects by phone, warm calls may be more comfortable than cold calls. Networking can be accomplished with one-on-one coffee dates rather than attending mixers filled with strangers. When you choose activities closer to your comfort zone, you'll be much more likely to actually engage in them.

- **Make a written plan that states exactly what you will do, how much of it, and when.** Plan your marketing activities just once, then do them many times. Saying you will "network" is not a plan. Writing that you will "attend one live networking event per week," then putting those dates on your calendar — that's a plan you can truly use.
- **Measure both your progress and your results, and re-evaluate your plan monthly.** Track your progress by noting which activities in your plan are completed each week. Then you can reward yourself for what you've done, or see when you need to allow more time for marketing. Set a goal each month for new prospects or new clients, so you'll have a benchmark to evaluate how well your plan is working.

You don't need to be a marketing expert to create an effective business-building plan. You just need to follow a few basic principles like those above. This time next month, you could be on track to having all the clients you want.

HERE IT IS AT LAST:
THE SECRET TO MARKETING

❖

Isn't that what every self-employed professional is really looking for — that one magic formula that will take the effort out of marketing and bring you all the clients you need, forever?

Searching for this marketing silver bullet, they read articles and books, take seminars and home-study courses, and hire consultants and coaches. And in the process, they learn about many, many so-called marketing secrets.

These "secrets" to marketing consist of supposedly surefire approaches like search engine optimization for your website, social media marketing, joining a leads group, sending postcards, and running pay-per-click ads. There are of course many more, and each of them is being touted by someone as the ultimate solution for marketing your business.

Trying to sort out the truth in these conflicting claims leaves you with three basic possibilities:

- All of this is nonsense; there is no secret to marketing.
- One of these approaches probably really is the secret, but since you have no way of knowing which one, you'd have to try them all.
- All of these probably are secrets for some people at some times, but none of them may be right for you.

No matter which of these points of view you take, the result is that none of these secrets are ultimately very helpful.

For many years, I've said that the real secret to marketing for self-employed professionals is choosing a set of simple, effective things to do, and doing them consistently.

That word "effective" can make this a bit tricky. You have to know what is effective in order for this secret to work for you. If you were to choose a set of completely ineffective things to do, this approach would fail.

But by "completely ineffective," I mean ideas like running a newspaper ad to market a management consulting business, or networking on Facebook in order to make more contacts with doctors, or sending out direct mail letters to attract psychotherapy patients. When the marketing tactics you pick are that far off base, no amount of consistency will make them work.

> With consistency and persistence, you can make even the most mildly effective marketing approaches pay off...

If you choose a set of activities that have any level of effectiveness, they will work if you do them consistently. Cold calling will work if you make enough calls. In-person networking will work if you attend events regularly and follow up with those you meet. Public speaking will work if you speak to audiences of a decent size on a regular basis.

With consistency and persistence, you can make even the most mildly effective marketing approaches pay off in the long run. But that qualifier "in the long run" is the catch. You don't want to wait that long. No one does.

Is there another layer to this secret that will make it all happen faster? Yes. Choose a target market that needs your services and can afford to pay for them, craft a message that market will respond to, choose a set of simple, effective approaches to reach that market, follow through on each approach, and spend enough time on your marketing to produce results.

Notice your emotional reaction to reading those words. They're not very exciting, are they? It sounds like work.

It would be much easier if the secret was something like search engine optimization, where you could pay someone else to do all the work and the clients would simply appear.

Or joining a leads group, where you could show up at a weekly meeting and the other members would hand you business. Or running pay-per-click ads, where you would never have to talk to people before they became your clients. But of course, none of these approaches really work that way.

Don't blame yourself for wanting to avoid hard work. It's human nature to look for the easy way out. But if you spend all your time searching for the effort-free way to market, you will end up making your job much harder.

Every time you try another new way to market but then don't follow through on it, or give up too soon to see results, you waste time and money, and lose momentum. By trying to avoid work, you actually create even more.

So instead of looking for a magic formula to avoid the work of marketing altogether, find ways to make it easier on yourself. Here are four suggestions that will help:

1. Choose a target market you enjoy spending time with, and whose issues and goals you care about.
2. Get help with crafting marketing messages if messaging isn't your strong point.
3. Use role models, recommended advisors, or a trusted system to identify only the best marketing approaches, then do what they advise.
4. Use the support of a buddy, coach, or success team to help you follow through on your plans, market consistently, and break through fear and procrastination.

***

Note that if the above are ways to make marketing easier, doing the opposite of any of these will make it harder. Refusing to choose a target market, for example. Or spending time and money marketing with a completely off-target message. Or trying flavor-of-the-week marketing tactics no successful person in your field ever uses. Or not doing enough marketing because it's scary. Or trying to do everything all on your own. Or continuing to chase after silver bullet solutions.

The secret to successful marketing for self-employed professionals is choosing a set of simple, effective things to do, and doing them consistently. The secret behind this secret is finding ways to make the process easier. And the secret behind *that* secret is to stop looking for another secret and get to work on implementing the first one.

PART III

❖

WHERE ARE YOU HEADED?
GOALS, PRIORITIES AND FOCUS

GET MORE CLIENTS BY DOING LESS

❖

I've been hearing from a lot of tired self-employed professionals lately. "I'm tired of going to networking events," they say, or, "I'm tired of always having to think up new stuff to post online." They're working pretty hard at marketing, it seems — networking, blogging, posting to social media, speaking, making calls, sending out e-mail blasts, and more.

When they don't get the results they want from marketing, professionals usually try to take on more. If their focus has been on in-person marketing, they begin marketing online. Or if they have been writing articles and blogging and being active on social media, they decide to start speaking and giving workshops. Or if they've been going to lots of events and lunches and coffee dates, they add in a call-mail-call campaign.

Huff, puff... it makes me tired just to write about all that activity.

What if the answer was actually to be found in the opposite direction? What if instead of doing more to get clients, you should really be doing less?

Here's an example of what I mean. A client I'll call Rhoda was trying to build her psychotherapy practice with a dozen different marketing approaches. She was going to professional meetings, posting flyers around her neighborhood, advertising in several directories, maintaining a Facebook page, trying to optimize her website, and more. She was tired, overwhelmed, and still didn't have enough clients.

I asked Rhoda where her best clients had come from so far — those who paid her full fee and continued to work with her over time. It turns out they had all been referrals from other professionals. I suggested that Rhoda stop everything she was currently doing about marketing, and concentrate on referral building. She was to identify a few categories of professionals who were likely to refer clients in her market niche, and get to know some people in those professions better.

When I checked in with Rhoda a few weeks later, she had already gotten some referrals from new people she had gotten to know. It was clear that if she kept working on building referral relationships with appropriate professionals, more clients would result. "Why didn't I ever do this before?" Rhoda said. "This is so much easier than all that other stuff I was doing, and it obviously works better."

> Are you tired of doing so much marketing? Maybe it's time to discover how you could do less.

Another client — I'll call him Doug — was seeking more small business clients for his IT consulting business. He was writing a blog and spending a lot of time on several social media platforms. When we first spoke, he was trying to decide whether to launch a podcast, offer a webinar series, or both.

"What's your follow-up strategy?" I asked Doug. He wasn't sure. I tried again: "Okay, how many prospects do you have in your pipeline?" He didn't know that either. In fact, a bit more probing determined that Doug didn't have a pipeline, or a follow-up strategy. He was simply trying to be more visible online, and hoping that as a result, clients who needed him would contact him.

My suggestion to Doug was that before he spent any more effort on becoming visible, he should put in place a strategy for identifying, capturing, and following up with likely prospects.

Doug decided to offer a free phone consultation to business owners who met a few qualifying criteria. He posted about his offer in his blog and on social media. One of his first free consultations turned into a new client, and two other consultations generated clients later on when Doug followed up with them. Doug never did launch a podcast or webinar series; he didn't need them.

A woman I'll call Mara was a student in one of my classes. She had diligently been attending several new networking events per week, and was regularly meeting many people. She asked me how she could find new places to network, because only a handful of the people she met had become clients so far. And maybe they could be breakfast meetings, because her calendar was already so full at lunch and in the evenings.

Mara was surprised — and relieved — when I suggested that finding even more places to network might not be the best approach. "What if you were to choose just a handful of those networking groups," I proposed, "go back to the same ones on a regular basis, and become better acquainted with the other members?" Mara agreed to try this out, focusing on those groups where she had found the highest concentration of people in her market niche.

I ran into Mara again at a speaking engagement some months later. "You were so right about networking," she told me. "When I stopped running around to all those different places, and became a regular, people started to recognize me, and then they started to do business with me."

Are you tired of doing so much marketing? Maybe it's time to discover how you could do less. Ask yourself, like Rhoda, what is the one thing you've done to market yourself so far that had the biggest impact. Could you do more of that?

Or, like Doug, determine how you can take better advantage of the visibility you already have. Or, like Mara, stop for a moment and wonder if there is a more effective way to employ the tactics you're already using.

Self-employed professionals do tend to work hard. But I'll bet you'd much rather work hard at your profession, and get paid for it, than to spend all your entrepreneurial energy getting clients in the first place.

MARKETING IN NEED OF FOCUS?
FOCUS YOUR BUSINESS

❖

"I'm having trouble building a website for my business," a student told me. "The web designer I'm working with says I'm trying to do too many things, and I shouldn't put it all on one site. But there are so many kinds of work I can do, and I don't want to limit myself."

When you have a problem like this, it affects more than just your website. Consider that when you choose a particular line of business to pursue, you aren't limiting yourself; you are packaging yourself.

The average citizen of the developed world sees or hears hundreds of marketing messages per day. If you want your marketing message to stand out, it must be brief, clear, and memorable. Giving people a long list of things to remember is a sure way to have them forget everything. You need to find one sentence, plus no more than three "labels" that describe what you do.

Here are some examples. I often introduce myself with: "I help self-employed professionals land more clients. I'm an author, speaker, and business coach." An image consultant I met said she "helps real people get dressed," by offering assistance with "colors, clothes and closets."

These three-item lists, along with a simple sentence, are easy to remember. Many people who learn about you will not be ready to do business with you right away, so you want them to remember you when they are ready. You also want them to be able to refer you to others.

If you're not convinced how important this tight focus is in marketing, consider one common way to promote your business -- introducing yourself at a networking event. If you introduce yourself as a graphic designer, desktop publisher, copywriter, art director, and production manager, people will go to sleep before you're through. But if you tell them, "I design and produce annual reports for corporate clients," they may even have a lead for you.

Marketing is not the only reason you need a narrow business focus. One of the most common mistakes small business owners make is to start off going in several directions at once. The start-up years of a business are stressful enough without diffusing your energies in this way.

> ...your business focus will often be a compromise between your personal desires and practical considerations. But don't compromise too far.

Having too many balls in the air will use up both time and money, the two most precious resources you have in business. The true path to success is to begin with a strong foundation in one area, then branch out to others as you become more established.

If you are having difficulty choosing where to focus, consider the problem from two different points of view. First:

- What type of work do you most want to do?
- What is the most satisfying and enjoyable?
- What will allow you to best honor your personal values, and work with people whose problems and goals you care about?

Second:

- What will allow you to make the kind of living you would like?

- Which markets most value the kind of work you want to do?
- Who can afford to pay what you need to charge?

As with many things in life, your business focus will often be a compromise between your personal desires and practical considerations. But don't compromise too far.

Look for ways to get most of what you want all in one place. For example, some self-employed professionals focus on offering their services to socially conscious companies, while others choose to pursue only clients who value quality work. Your best bet is to follow the path that you are personally the most excited about.

HOW MANY CLIENTS DO YOU REALLY NEED

❖

When I speak on the topic of reliable ways to get clients, I often suggest ezines, blogging, white papers, ebooks, mini-courses, and other forms of free information as a vehicle for communicating your expertise to clients and building their trust. "But people are so overwhelmed with information," members of the audience frequently ask me, "What's the point of publishing more stuff no one has the time to read?"

I certainly agree that our prospects are suffering from information overload, and that it's harder than ever to get their attention. But in my view, that's even more of a reason to provide them with useful information instead of merely sales pitches.

When people don't have the time to look at everything that crosses their screen, which are they going to choose to read — a blog post that might help them solve a problem, or a promo email that's trying to sell them something?

Clearly, when time is short, your prospects will choose to spend it in ways that provide a higher return. So the more value your email, article, or web page can deliver, the more likely it is that someone will take a moment to look at it.

It seems that many of those asking this question had been reading reports that fewer people were reading ezines and blogs these days, that the number of free ebooks and mini-courses had risen dramatically, and so on. And it's true that for mega-marketers who deal with large numbers of customers, these trends can signal a significant problem.

But if you're a self-employed professional like the average *Get Clients Now!* reader, I don't think there's that much cause for alarm. The reason is simple: how many clients do you really need?

If you're a corporate consultant, you might need only two or three new clients per year. A graphic designer might need twelve or fifteen. If you're a life coach, you might need twenty.

It's a different story for people who sell products and low-cost classes. They need hundreds or thousands of customers per year to turn a profit. But when you're selling your own professional services, and your average client pays you $2,500-$25,000 over a year's time, you simply don't need that many of them.

> ...advice that may be on target for a product-based business with a large customer base can be totally misleading for a solo professional.

If you send your ezine to 2,000 people and only 400 of them open it, is this really a problem when you're only looking for twelve clients this year?

Let's say 1,000 people visit your website each month, but only 5% of them download your white paper. Should you truly be worried if you're only seeking two new clients? The number of prospects who are taking the time to look at your information in both these examples seems quite sufficient to me.

Just as with so many other aspects of marketing, advice that may be on target for a product-based business with a large customer base can be totally misleading for a solo professional. So please don't stop publishing — plenty of your prospective clients are still out there reading your words.

After all, you read this, didn't you?

TOO BUSY TO GET CLIENTS

❖

"I don't have enough clients," one of my students told me. "I'd love to put more effort into marketing, but I'm so busy, I don't have the time."

This person's dilemma might seem humorous, but it's no joke. I've heard this complaint repeatedly from self-employed professionals. You'd think the solution would be easy — just drop whatever else you're doing and spend more time on getting clients. But making that adjustment is often not so simple.

Here are five too-busy-to-get-clients situations that you may encounter, and what you can do about them.

1. You're too busy serving existing clients. This is probably the most common reason named by self-employed professionals for not spending time marketing. On the surface, it seems like a good excuse. If you're busy with paying work, why should you take time away to market?

But the work eventually comes to an end, and there you are with no new clients lined up. Now you have time to market, but it always takes a while to land something new. Meanwhile, there's no money coming in.

The only way to break this feast-or-famine cycle is to go shopping before the cupboard is bare.

Even when you have plenty of work, set aside time on a weekly basis to focus on marketing for new clients. When agreeing on project or appointment schedules with an existing client, factor in this set-aside time, just as you would if it was another client you were serving simultaneously. Your business deserves the same kind of care and attention you give to your clients' businesses.

163

2. You're too busy working for peanuts, or even for free.
One reason you might have trouble finding time to market is
that you're working too much for too little. Perhaps your fees
are too low, you are giving away too many free consultations
or sample sessions, or you are
doing too much work "on spec."
Or perhaps you are spending
many hours volunteering for a
trade association or nonprofit.

Try keeping a work diary for
two weeks, where you record
every hour you spend working
on other peoples' projects and
what you got paid for them. If
you don't like what you see, start
making some changes.

> Be honest with
> yourself — when are
> you networking with
> important business
> contacts and when
> are you just
> socializing?

Place a ceiling on the amount
of time you give away for free. Set your rates based on the
true cost of doing business, which includes unpaid time spent
on marketing and management. Don't let under-earning rob
you of the time you need to market your business.

3. You're too busy networking. Not all networking
"counts" as marketing. Attending meetings and workshops,
having coffee or lunch, and spending time on Facebook,
Twitter, or LinkedIn can have a worthwhile business
purpose… or be an enormous waste of your precious
marketing time.

Be honest with yourself — when are you networking with
important business contacts and when are you just
socializing? Limit your business networking to people who
are either in your target market, or who come in frequent
contact with your target market.

Sure, anyone might refer you a client, but the point is to spend the majority of your time with those who are most likely to either become prospects or refer them. Reduce the time you invest in networking to an amount on which you might reasonably expect to see a profitable return.

4. You're too busy marketing unproductively.

Networking isn't the only type of marketing that can consume more time than it's worth. Another common misuse of time is putting all your effort into filling the pipeline with new prospects, then rarely following up with them after the initial contact. Or, focusing on making cold approaches by phone or email to people who have never heard of you, instead of using your network to ask for introductions and referrals.

If you feel like you're spending a lot of time on marketing already, but still don't have all the clients you need, you probably need to revisit your approach. What do you think are the three most effective ways for a business like yours to get clients? Now, are those three ways how you've been spending the majority of your marketing time? If not, change your strategy.

5. You're too busy with a day job, school, or family responsibilities.

Trying to squeeze a business into an already full life doesn't always work. It's a common mistake to consider only the time you'll need to serve clients, and not the time needed to get them in the first place. But to run a successful business, marketing has to be part of the picture.

It may be that your part-time business will need longer to get off the ground than you thought. If you don't like that option, perhaps you can negotiate fewer hours at your job, take some time off from work or school, or share family responsibilities with someone else.

Don't get discouraged; most new business owners face this same issue. We like to believe that time is infinitely expandable, but it's not so. When you add time into one area of life, it must come from another.

The next time you find yourself thinking you are too busy to get clients, think again. If you don't have enough time for marketing, something about your business needs to change. Stop what you're doing, and take the time to figure out what it is.

THERE'S MORE THAN ONE WAY
TO GROW A BUSINESS

❖

Every entrepreneur wants to earn more from his or her business. When you ask business owners how they plan to meet that goal, they usually talk about doing a better job at marketing or doing more of it. But in fact, there are many ways to go about growing a business. Here are five of the best strategies for any business to consider.

1. Find a bigger market. What needs does your business fill for your clients? Can you identify another group of people with those same needs? If you can, there is a brand new market just waiting to find out about your business.

Here's an example: a child care center started out by aiming their advertising at parents. The center was doing well, but their marketing costs were high. Then they learned that many companies wanted to provide child care for employees, but couldn't afford to open their own center.

By contracting directly with these companies to care for their employees' children, the center was quickly filled to capacity, and dramatically decreased its marketing costs.

2. Find a richer market. If you find yourself struggling to sell to people who often can't afford you, look for another market that can pay what you need to charge. Many companies that do business with nonprofits discover that they also need to have a few corporate clients, in order to compensate for the lower rates nonprofits frequently require.

The same is true when you work with individual consumers. If the group you most love to serve is in a lower income bracket, spend some of your time marketing to a higher income group as well. If you can charge higher fees to the group who can afford it, do so.

3. Build a back end. It costs less and takes less time to sell something new to the clients you already have. If you're not sure what this might be, try asking your clients what other needs they have. An acupuncturist, for example, could also sell herbal supplements or educational books and CD's.

> Be creative in thinking about growth. If you run out of ideas, remember — ask your clients!

Consultants often find that clients have many other needs, once they begin working on a project. If a client needs something that you can't provide yourself, consider subcontracting the business to someone else and taking a percentage, or collecting a fee for making a referral.

4. Change your pricing. Any marketing expert will tell you that pricing is magic, not science. When you lower prices, sales usually go up. When you raise them, costs usually go down. The "perfect" price is the one that makes you the most money, but how do you find it?

The place to start is by doing some modeling. Calculate the size of your average sale, then estimate how much each sale costs you to make. (A good reference book on writing a business plan can help.) Then, play with the numbers: see what happens to your profit as you raise or lower your prices and estimate how your sales volume might go up or down.

When you model, you're just guessing, of course, but many entrepreneurs are surprised to see that lowering their prices can sometimes bring more profit. Or by combining a price increase with idea #2 above, you could potentially make more money from fewer sales.

5. Find a strategic partner. Is there a company out there who you could partner with to gain access to their market? Imagine what your earnings would be like if Dell or Apple included your product or service as part of the package with every computer they sold.

Take a look at the leaders in your marketplace and see if there isn't someone whose product or service is a natural companion to yours. Partnering can work between small companies, too. A chiropractor and a massage therapist can share space and exchange clients. A professional organizer and a computer consultant can team up to help clients organize information.

Be creative in thinking about growth. If you run out of ideas, remember — ask your clients! They know better than anyone what more your business could be doing to serve them.

DO YOU KNOW WHO YOUR CLIENTS ARE?

❖

If you haven't clearly defined the target market for your business as a self-employed professional, you may actually be preventing yourself from getting clients. I often hear professionals say they don't want to "limit" themselves by narrowing their marketing focus to a specific group. They are afraid they will lose out on potential business. But the truth is that defining a target market doesn't limit your marketing; it aims it.

When clients show up at your door, you can always choose to work with them regardless of whether they belong in your target market. But to go out and find new clients on your own, you need to have an organizing principle for your outreach efforts. The universe is simply too big to market effectively to everyone in it.

Here are four more reasons why choosing a target market is so essential.

1. Targeting allows you to position yourself in the marketplace. With a particular type of client in mind, you can create an identity that appeals to exactly that group. A clear marketing identity will enable you to project a consistent image to those you wish to reach, and take advantage of the market appeal of factors like exclusivity and specialization.

Clients prefer to work with someone whose specializes in their industry or type of project. You'll close more sales as a specialist than as a jack-of-all-trades.

2. Marketing to a defined group of clients will cost you less in both time and money. You will be able to locate leads and reach out to prospects much more easily, because you will be able to quickly identify who they are. With significantly less effort, you will be able to find places — both online and offline -- where clients gather, call them, write them, and meet with them. Instead of being paralyzed by all the possible places you could network, or prospect, or speak, or advertise, you'll know exactly which venues are most likely to pay off.

3. You can get to know your market better. When marketing to a finite universe, it becomes much more possible to meet members of your client base in person, build referral relationships, network via social media, and increase word-of-mouth.

> Defining a target market is not quite as simple as saying it is "anyone who needs my services."

You'll be able to learn more about your market's problems and concerns, and can tailor your services and your marketing messages more closely to match what they are seeking. You'll have a much easier time building the know-like-and-trust factor that encourages prospects to buy.

4. Targeting makes it possible to use attraction marketing. Broadcasting your marketing message to a mass audience is prohibitively expensive, no matter how you do it. Media advertising, trade show booths, direct mail, and publicity campaigns can reach thousands of people, but the cost can exceed the return.

When you limit your audience to a group you can more easily reach, you can attract them through the lower-cost attraction-based strategies of personal networking, referral-building, writing, and speaking.

***

Defining a target market is not quite as simple as saying it is "anyone who needs my services." That won't help you locate prospective clients, tell others who your ideal clients are, or even identify them when you happen to run into them. You need to describe your desired market with labels or categories, the more specific the better. That way you can look them up or seek them out.

For example, "busy professionals" or "midsize organizations" are fair definitions, but "upscale baby-boomers" or "growing high-tech companies" would be better, because they further qualify your target.

Categories like "professional women in health care" or "financial services firms in the Seattle area" are excellent, because you can find prospects that match these definitions in a directory or on a membership roster. You can also describe exactly who you'd most like to have referred to you.

Beware the temptation to leave your target market definition broad. When your definition is too general, your client universe remains overly large and your efforts and message will be diffused. You would be better served by carefully defining two or three different, but specific, target markets to approach than by trying to come up with a one-size-fits-all definition of who your clients are.

When there are many possibilities for a target market, who should you choose? I believe the most important factor is to identify a group of people you truly care about, and who you want to spend your time with. The more you enjoy interacting with a specific group, the easier your marketing to that group will be.

But be sure you are choosing a target market that can provide a sustainable stream of revenue. The ideal target group is one to which you already have some established connections, can easily afford to pay what you charge, and will lead to repeat business over time.

HOW TO TELL CLIENTS
YOU HAVE WHAT THEY NEED

❖

Do you know *why* clients should hire you? Yes? That's an excellent beginning. But it's not enough for you to know why clients should hire you — the clients need to know it, too. It's hard enough to find clients without also having to educate them on why they would want to work with someone like you in the first place. The needs your service fills must be important enough that prospective clients are already looking for a solution like yours before they hear about you.

Let's say you are an accountant looking for more year-round clients in the small business market. You want to help business owners stay on top of their numbers on a regular basis, not just at tax time. So, you begin advertising your firm as offering "full-service accounting."

But do small business owners know they need full-service accounting? Typically, no. When they hear the word "accounting," it's most likely to translate in their minds to "bookkeeping" and "tax preparation." If those needs are already handled, why would they need an accountant?

What you know that many of your potential clients don't is that, as an accountant, you are qualified to advise them on many areas of their business: budgeting, cash flow, investment strategies, advance tax planning, business financing, expansion plans, incorporation, retirement and estate planning, and more. But unless you speak directly to those specific needs, most prospective clients won't make the connection on their own.

Find out what the "hot buttons" are for people in your target market. What do they perceive to be the greatest problems they face, or the biggest goals they wish to achieve?

Ask these questions of the people you serve and the other professionals who serve them. Read trade literature or special interest publications and educate yourself on the key issues in your marketplace.

When you have a clear picture of what your target market is truly looking for, you'll be able to package your service as a solution. Design all your marketing and sales tools — elevator speech, website, social media profiles, blog, brochure, telemarketing script, sales presentation — to show how what you do addresses the specific hot buttons you identified.

> ...the way a service provider gets in the door is to solve the "presenting problem" of the client... Once you are on board and working for the client, you will no doubt uncover all sorts of other issues that need to be addressed.

Make sure when you describe your services to potential clients that you're using words they will recognize, rather than your own industry's jargon.

Perhaps you know that as a marketing communications consultant, you are qualified to write web copy, brochures, sales letters, and advertisements. But your prospective clients may think the person they need to hire provides "copywriting" rather than "marketing communications." They may not even recognize that your stated specialty is exactly what they need.

You will probably have much more success in connecting the dots between what you offer and what your clients need if you focus on describing the results you deliver instead of the services you provide. "I write web copy, sales letters, and ads" is much more understandable to the person on the street than "I'm a marketing communications consultant," or even "I offer copywriting services."

Seasoned professionals know that the way a service provider gets in the door is to solve the "presenting problem" of the client. When potential clients have already identified that they have a pressing need that you can fill, you always stand a much better chance of being hired.

Once you are on board and working for the client, you will no doubt uncover all sorts of other issues that need to be addressed. And since you are already on the scene, building rapport and trust, of course they will retain you to help resolve those problems.

This sequence is common for any service business professional, from hypnotherapists to graphic designers. The client hires the designer to create business cards; then the designer discovers the client doesn't have a logo.

When the designer shows the client how much more impressive the business cards would be with a custom logo on them, the client agrees to pay for one. But if the designer had approached that person about creating a logo, the client would likely have refused. In the client's mind, it was business cards that were needed.

Don't worry if the most pressing issues your prospects seem to be facing aren't the ones you think are the most important. If you attract clients by marketing to their perceived needs, you'll create plenty of opportunities to explore other ways you can assist them. But if you market something they don't yet know they want, you may never get to have the conversation.

LACK OF CLIENTS
ISN'T ALWAYS THE PROBLEM

❖

When you're just starting out in business, it's a safe bet that you need more clients. But what if you've been up and running for a while, and you're still not making as much money as you would like? You may be in the habit of thinking that attracting new clients will be the answer, but this isn't always the case.

There are many reasons why a self-employed professional might not be earning enough, but the reasons typically fall into four categories: not enough revenue, not enough profit, not enough clients, or not enough time.

Start by looking at your gross revenue — the total amount your clients pay you over the course of a year. How does it compare to others in the same line of business? Ask some trusted colleagues or check with your professional association for any statistics they may have.

What percentage of your gross revenue remains after you cover your cost of sales? This is your gross profit. As a service business, you may have no cost of sales. If, however, you are accepting credit cards, using an online payment system like PayPal, or selling products such as books or courses, your payment processing fees and costs of producing your inventory need to be deducted from your earnings before making other calculations.

Now deduct your business expenses from your gross profit. What percentage of gross profit remains? Is this a typical percentage for your industry?

Try to gather comparable data from colleagues, your professional association, or a published source like Dun & Bradstreet's "Industry Norms & Key Business Ratios" (available through many libraries). If you can't find appropriate guidance from any of those sources, make an estimate by comparing your profit margin (net income divided by gross profit) to a desired goal of 70%.

1. Not enough revenue. If your gross revenue seems low for your industry, but your profit margin is at least 70%, and you have about as many clients as you can comfortably serve, concentrate on increasing your revenue, rather than trying to improve your profit margin or just bring in new clients.

> Look for clients with deeper pockets who will hire you for higher dollar volume engagements or purchase more expensive offerings.

Consider raising your rates, which may mean finding a market that is willing to pay more. Look for clients with deeper pockets who will hire you for higher dollar volume engagements or purchase more expensive offerings. Think about hiring more administrative help, which would free up more of your time to charge out at professional rates.

You might also consider increasing your passive income by selling products created by you or others, reselling some of your existing work, or licensing a process you have developed.

2. Not enough profit. If you are spending more than 30% of your gross profit on business expenses like overhead costs or marketing, work on improving your profits. Look for ways to cut expenses by reducing your overhead, or focusing on your most profitable line of business.

In addition, if more than 15% of your gross profit is spent on marketing alone (assuming you are already past the start-up phase), consider cutting back on paid advertising or mailings, and using marketing strategies that focus on building referrals or attracting clients through writing and speaking. Seek out clients who will give you repeat business or long-term contracts.

3. Not enough clients. Low revenue combined with not enough paying work to keep you busy means you really don't have enough customers. If you don't have a marketing plan, it's time to create one. Focus your plan on the most attractive services you have to offer and the most lucrative market, rather than diffusing your energy by marketing several different service lines to more than one type of customer.

If you already have a marketing plan, but it's not paying off, you may need to break into a new market, look for a more appealing way to package your services, or form an alliance with someone who can send a steady stream of business your way.

4. Not enough time. It's possible that you simply don't have enough time to earn more revenue. When you are consistently spending over 25 hours per week serving clients, with more potential clients in the pipeline than you can realistically serve, it's time to hire admin or marketing help, or bring in a junior partner.

If you're not ready to take that step, think about subcontracting work to a trusted associate, and keeping a percentage of their billings.

***

In reading the suggestions above, you may have discovered that you don't have enough information to diagnose your earnings problem. There are six statistics every self-employed professional should know: revenue, expenses, profit margin, number of clients, average sale amount, and amount of time spent doing paying work. If you don't have the answers, start tracking these measurements today.

IN MARKETING, ONE SIZE DOES NOT FIT ALL

❖

Imagine that you went shopping to buy yourself a new shirt, and the salesperson offered you a garment three sizes too big, saying, "This is one of our most popular colors." Or showed you a shirt in a child's size, telling you, "This style is new this season." You'd probably think the salesperson was crazy, right? And you certainly wouldn't trust his or her judgment about what shirt might be right for you.

Unfortunately, this sort of thing goes on with marketing all the time. Without asking you a single question about your situation, an acquaintance describes the latest marketing idea they heard about, and urges you to try it.

Or a workshop leader who knows nothing about your business explains the best way to market your services and recommends you adopt it. Or a consultant advises you to use a specific marketing approach with almost no understanding of your business.

It can be tempting to follow recommendations like these. After all, these folks sound so sure of themselves, and perhaps you feel on shaky ground where marketing is concerned. Maybe you should just take the advice of people who seem to know more. Or maybe not.

Maybe marketing needs to fit you every bit as much as a shirt does. If it's too big or too small, casual when you need something businesslike, or designed for a party when you're planning a workout, it won't do you any good.

Here are four different types of "size" to help you measure the fit of your marketing.

1. Marketing a professional service is not the same as marketing a product. Products are tangible; you can see them, touch them, maybe even taste them before you buy. Services are intangible. You can't experience them until they are demonstrated. Because a service is intangible, until it is performed for you, you have no idea how it will turn out, whether you will like it, or whether it will work for your problem, situation, or opportunity.

Therefore, when clients purchase a service for the first time, they must rely on their judgment about the person delivering it. They must trust you. Trust is built through positive experiences over time, by referrals and recommendations from reliable sources, and credibility-boosters like speaking, writing, or media stories.

> ...the key is to be realistic. What can you actually execute well with the time and money you have available?

Marketing your services with any approach that doesn't build trust (or may even harm it), is a bad fit. Examples are mile-long sales pages filled with over-the-top hype, subscribing prospects to an email list without explicit permission, or ads offering low prices and deep discounts. These are tactics that sell products; that's why you see them so often. But that doesn't mean you should copy them.

2. Small business marketing is different than big business marketing. Big businesses have marketing departments and sales departments performing different functions. They have full-time staff dedicated to marketing and sales. They have substantial marketing budgets, and they can afford to invest in name recognition.

You, however, as a small business owner, must manage both marketing and sales, and that's only part of your job. If you're a solo business, you have to actually perform all the work of sales and marketing, too, except for those portions you might be able to contract out. Your budget doesn't allow for marketing approaches that only result in name recognition; you need your marketing to turn into closed sales.

Bad fits for a small business include promotion and advertising just to "get your name out there," selling strategies that require making dozens of phone calls per day to pay off, and maintaining multiple websites and social networking profiles to increase your online visibility.

To find approaches with a better fit, the key is to be realistic. What can you actually execute well with the time and money you have available? Successful small business owners often rely on low-cost, low-tech strategies like personal networking to build their contacts and referrals, public speaking, or pursuing high-value clients by researching contacts or leads and contacting them directly.

3. One-to-one marketing doesn't use the same tactics as one-to-many marketing. How many clients do you need to have a successful year? Three, or three hundred? The answer makes a world of difference to the sort of marketing that fits your business best.

When your business consists of a handful of large, ongoing contracts, one-to-one marketing is a perfect fit. Your marketing plan might include no more than attending or presenting at professional meetings, following up consistently with a small group of prospects, and lunch with colleagues.

But if your business is made up of many small sales to a large number of people, one-to-many marketing is called for.

You'll need approaches that allow you to become known to a substantial audience, such as publishing an ezine or blog, public speaking, or a strong social media presence.

4. B2B marketing isn't the same as B2C marketing, and SB2SB marketing is its own category. B2B stands for business to business, B2C means business to consumer, and SB2SB is small business to small business, a lesser known classification, but a rapidly growing group.

Depending on which of these three labels fits your target market best, you might focus your social media marketing efforts on LinkedIn (best for B2B) or Facebook (best for B2C or SB2SB). You might include cold calling in your marketing plan (B2B or SB2SB) or leave it alone (B2C). You might do best by giving presentations to corporate audiences (B2B or B2C), or to small business networks (SB2SB).

Clearly, knowing where you fit among these different marketing "sizes" is essential to choosing the right marketing approaches. Are you a small business marketing B2B services one-to-one? A small business marketing B2C services one-to-many? Or perhaps you need a custom size.

If you truly want your marketing to fit your business, you'd better know your measurements. And, when someone tries to tell you how to market, they'd better know your measurements, too.

CRACKING THE BILLABLE HOURS CEILING

❖

How many of you made as much money as you wanted to last year? Don't be shy; raise your hands. Hmm, I don't see too many hands out there. What would you say is the cause of this gap between your goals and your earnings?

While you could certainly name the economy or inadequate marketing as the culprit, I'd like to suggest a third alternative. It may be the constraints of the billable hours model that keep you from your financial goals.

Let's face it, there are only so many hours you can actually bill to clients. In most professions, it's impossible to bill 100% of your time. Consultants, for example, report being able to bill only 50-80% of a forty-hour week.

You can only raise your rates so high and still find enough customers. And if you spend more time on marketing, that's less time you have available to bill.

But there's a way out of this trap. No matter what type of business you're in, you can use intellectual property to crack the billable hours ceiling. Here are just some of the ways to start tapping into this resource today.

1. Package your process. What if every time you began work with a new client, they paid an up-front fee before you spent even one hour with them? If you sell a process rather than your time, clients will pay for access to your previously developed materials. Examples are workbooks, assessments, templates, games, self-paced programs, and train-the-trainer packages.

2. Give a class. When you assemble a group of people to learn together, you can earn more per hour than working with them separately. Classes can be given at your office, at a rented (or borrowed) facility, on the phone, by video, by email, or online. Your market for classes is not just your clients — think about what you could teach your colleagues as well.

3. Record an audio or video. The simplest way to make recordings is to capture your live classes or speaking engagements on audio or video. Then make your unedited recordings available immediately as digital downloads or burn them to CD's or DVD's.

> If you've been counting on hourly fees for your entire income, you may be surprised at the impact developing your intellectual property will have.

More polished recordings can be made with the help of a local studio or hired multimedia editor, or you can learn to do this yourself with the right equipment and software.

4. Write a workbook, how-to-guide, or ebook. Short publications like these are easily within your reach, even if you don't consider yourself a writer. A twenty-page guide might have as few as 4,000 words in it. If you've written four articles or blog posts aimed at prospective clients, you may have already written this much. Collections of how-to material are perfect for ebooks, which cost you nothing to print.

5. Author a book. This might seem an impossible task, but if you write one page a day, five days a week, at the end of a year you'll have a full-length book. If writing isn't your strong point, find an editor, ghost writer, or even a co-author who has the skills you lack. You don't have to wait until your book is finished to start selling excerpts as articles and white papers.

6. Market other people's products. If you don't yet have your own product, don't let that stop you. You can begin earning passive income by selling other people's books and audio/video, becoming a reseller for software or assessment tools, licensing someone else's process, or joining affiliate programs.

Any of the products listed above can be marketed via activities you are already engaged in: conversations with prospects and clients, your blog or ezine, speaking engagements, and on your website.

If you've been counting on hourly fees for your entire income, you may be surprised at the impact developing your intellectual property will have. It will add not only to your revenue, but also your professional credibility. And when funds are tight, you will find that prospects who hesitate to pay for individual service will still purchase classes and information products.

HOW CAN I GROW
MY ONE-PERSON BUSINESS?

❖

If you've been operating a successful professional services business as a solopreneur, it can be a smart move to leverage your experience, contacts, and track record in the industry by adding other professionals to your team. Managing a multi-person firm will allow you to land contracts that other people can fulfill, and you'll start to make money while you sleep.

Making the transition from self-employed professional to managing partner, however, also has drawbacks. You will need to take on added responsibilities in management, administration, and marketing, which in turn will reduce the amount of time you have available to work on client projects yourself. You may find yourself spending considerably more time landing and managing contracts than you do working on them. Be sure that this change in focus is desirable for you before taking the leap.

If you think you're ready to graduate from solopreneur to CEO, the best place to begin is with a strategic plan. What sort of personnel do you plan to add? Will they be other professionals who do exactly the same type of work as you? Or will their skills complement yours to expand your company's capabilities as well as its capacity? How fast do you want to grow, in terms of personnel, revenue, and client base? What would you like to see by the end of this year, next year, five years from now?

Before you bring in any new contracts, start building your team. Your smartest first hire might be an administrative assistant or virtual assistant, rather than another professional. Having someone else to do administrative work will free up more of your time for billable work and business development. You might decide to hire someone part-time who could later grow into a full-time employee.

To bring other professionals into your firm, you probably want to start out by offering them "associate" status, even if you think you eventually might want partners. This will give you a chance to evaluate how well you work together, and whether the quality of their work is up to your standards, before making any long-term commitments.

The best financial arrangement is to pay associates as subcontractors rather than employees. You have no obligation to pay your subcontractors unless you have work for them, and don't need to withhold taxes or offer benefits. If your associates continue to also serve their own clients, and don't work out of your office, you may choose to keep them on as independent contractors indefinitely.

> Growing your business in this way… can be a wise long-term strategy, as it can not only increase your profits, but also help to make your company saleable…

When you are an associate's only client, however, it may become necessary to hire him or her as an employee to comply with IRS rules. You can still hire employee associates on an hourly basis, and only pay them when work is available. In either case, be sure there is a written agreement between you that spells out expectations.

With one or more associates lined up, you're ready to land the first contract for your newly expanded firm. This may be a project that you also work on, or business you develop for your associates alone. It's typical for a firm to keep anywhere from 15 to 30% of the revenue generated by an associate's work. (When associates are employees, the "house" percentage is often higher.) If you bill your client $100 per hour, for example, you might pay an associate $70-85.

Prepare for your new status by beginning to position your business as a firm instead of a person. This may mean changing your business name as well as revising your marketing materials. A name change may be as simple as adding "Associates" or "Group" to your own name. Or you may wish to choose a new name to represent your expanded enterprise.

Give yourself a job title, such as "President," "Principal," or "Senior Consultant," and add it to your business cards. Update your website and marketing materials to reflect the expanded capabilities of your firm.

Before offering an associate the opportunity to become a partner and share in the overall profits of the firm, make sure he or she has the ability to also bring in business for the company. Partnerships where only one of the principals lands all the business often don't succeed because the partnership feels unequal.

If you don't plan to offer partnership to your associates, they may choose to move on after a time. This is a normal transition that you should be prepared for. Make sure that your associate agreement covers issues such as giving notice, competition, and confidentiality, so that you won't be unduly harmed when an associate decides to leave.

Growing your business in this way — if it suits your skills and personal desires — can be a wise long-term strategy, as it can not only increase your profits, but also help to make your company saleable when you eventually decide to retire.

IF YOU AREN'T SEEING RESULTS YET, IS YOUR MARKETING ON TRACK?

❖

Many *Get Clients Now!* readers who plan their marketing with the 28-Day Program in the book struggle with the question of how to know they made the right choices about which marketing strategies to employ. No matter which techniques you choose, it can take time for them to pay off.

Direct contact and follow-up tactics, like sending emails or letters and placing phone calls, can require repeated contacts to have an effect. Networking and referral-building activities depend on nurturing relationships, and results aren't typically produced overnight. Public speaking engagements require lead time to set up and follow-up contacts to close sales. And so on.

When you are using these strategies for the first time in a focused, organized way, you haven't yet seen them produce clients. So, it's natural to start second-guessing your decisions and question your marketing plan. After all, you're putting in a lot of work, and if you don't see an increase in sales immediately, you may begin to wonder if you are on the right track.

In the book, I've given you a system to make these choices carefully. But you don't have to just take it on faith that my system works. Here are three ways to reassure yourself that your plan is going to pay off, if you give it the right amount of time or effort.

1. Ask for evidence. Contact the most successful self-employed professional you know, whether that's someone in your field or another service provider who serves a similar market. Ask that person where his or her clients came from in the early years of business. Then ask where they come from now. Compare the strategies that worked for him or her with what you are using. If you model your plan after a winner, you'll win too.

2. Run the numbers. If you follow your plan for 28 days, how many potential clients will you make contact with? Thirty? Sixty? One hundred? How many of those are likely to have enough interest in your service to take time for a conversation about it? Three? Six? Ten? Now of that group, how many sales can you close? One? Two? Three or four? And how many sales do you need this month? This type of reality check can convince you that your plan makes statistical sense.

> ...the mysterious phenomenon of achieving results seemingly unconnected to your efforts... isn't some woo-woo belief in marketing magic. It's simply the natural outcome of an increased level of activity.

3. Count on the Persistence Effect. In Chapter 5 of *Get Clients Now!*, I talk about the mysterious phenomenon of achieving results seemingly unconnected to your efforts. This isn't some woo-woo belief in marketing magic. It's simply the natural outcome of an increased level of activity. If you persist in making more calls, attending more events, or talking to more people, you will increase the number of calls you receive, referrals you get, and people who know about you. These new and varied contacts will ultimately translate to more business.

Remember that one of the principles of my system is that it doesn't matter so much what you choose as it does *that* you choose. If you diagnose where your marketing needs help, then pick a set of simple, effective things to do about it and do those things consistently for 28 days, you'll be taking action about marketing in a focused, organized way. And that's what being on track looks like.

WANT MORE CLIENTS? JUST SAY NO!

❖

Much of the popular wisdom about how to succeed as a self-employed professional seems to center around saying yes. You'll hear that you're supposed to market yourself constantly in as many different ways as possible, network with everyone you can find, and take as many clients as possible in order to increase your earnings. The implication is that you should say yes to every opportunity.

But it hasn't been my experience that pursuing all opportunities is the true path to success. In fact, my own success increased dramatically when I started saying no more often.

Saying yes to everything is like opening too many windows on your computer. Eventually you run out of resources and you crash. When you say yes to every suggestion, request, or invitation, you are letting other people's agendas drive your business. Saying no can put you in charge instead.

Here are six examples of situations where you may want to consider saying no.

1. New clients who don't fit into your niche. When business is scarce, it's tempting to take anything you can get. For a one-time or short-term project, working with a client outside your target market or specialty may not harm you. But making a practice of taking any business that shows up will get in the way of establishing your reputation and referral base.

These "outsider" clients won't lead to the targeted referrals or testimonials that will build your business. And they can take a lot more energy to serve, because you may need to learn on the job, scramble to assemble needed resources, or do work you simply don't enjoy much. Sticking to your niche, on the other hand, will lead to more business of the kind you really want to have.

2. Networking with people who have no connection to your niche. Your networking time is precious. Say no to attending events that will attract few people from your target market, or to meeting with people whose niche has no relation to yours.

Just because someone invites you to a meeting or coffee doesn't mean you have to go. Don't worry, you'll have plenty more invitations to choose from in the future. Plus, you should be spending some time making your own invitations to folks solidly within your niche, who will be much more likely to bring you business.

> Watch out for prospects who want to meet with you multiple times, see several proposals, or require a detailed response to a complex RFP before agreeing to work with you.

3. Clients who take more effort to pursue than their business is worth. Watch out for prospects who want to meet with you multiple times, see several proposals, or require a detailed response to a complex RFP before agreeing to work with you. Even when you ultimately land the contract, it may cost you far too much unpaid time. And clients who are so demanding before they hire you may be even worse to actually work for.

4. People and organizations who ask for your time but do nothing for you. Serving as a volunteer in order to give back to your community is a worthwhile activity in itself. But volunteering your time with the primary intent to market your business only pays off when the recipients of your largesse provide the promotional consideration they promised.

Beware of offers like online communities who award you a slot as an "expert" required to provide answers to questions, original blog posts, or downloadable tools for free, but can't deliver you the traffic they promised. Or community organizations who ask you to serve in your professional capacity pro bono, but never so much as acknowledge you in their newsletter.

5. Ads, promotional schemes, and exhibit space that don't fit your budget. The moment you hang out your shingle as a business owner, you become a prime target for people selling online and print ads, directory listings, search engine optimization, social media management, and trade show exhibits. Their offers may be appealing, especially if you're feeling a bit desperate for business. But for the solo self-employed professional, these approaches rarely pay back the required investment.

Consider this — if these promotional avenues were as valuable as the offers say, would they really need to have an army of commissioned salespeople pushing them on you? Before enrolling in any paid promotional scheme, compare its total cost to the value of closed sales you could conservatively expect to gain as a result. Make your own estimates; don't just accept what the salesperson says. Then say no to any offer that may cost you more than it brings in.

6. Flavor-of-the-month marketing approaches. Every time you turn around, it seems that someone has a new marketing idea for you. If you're not seeing immediate results from what you're already doing, it may be appealing to try something new. But keep in mind that every marketing strategy takes consistency and persistence to pay off.

When you drop what you're doing to try something new, you may lose out on both the benefit of what you were doing before and the new approach you're trying now, because you'll have given neither of them the attention and longevity they truly require.

Here's the bottom line. If you've ever felt like you were being pulled in a dozen different directions by the requirements of marketing your business, the solution may be right in front of you. Just say no to invitations, offers, and demands that serve the needs of other people better than they do your own.

MORE MONEY
OR THE PURSUIT OF HAPPINESS?

❖

We self-employed professionals are constantly faced with difficult choices about how to best grow our businesses. Should I pursue this line of business or that one? Would it serve me better to choose Niche A or Niche B? Shall I spend my time building a relationship with Client X or Client Y?

Often, these questions hinge on what we perceive as the most desirable result. If we value potential earnings more highly, we select a course of action that will lead to more money. If we are more concerned with our personal fulfillment, we follow a path that we believe will be more satisfying. Surprisingly often, these possible choices point in opposite directions. We find ourselves having to choose between higher earnings and greater happiness.

Or at least, that's what we think.

A client of mine who worked as a marketing consultant was presented with two potential projects — one with a large law firm specializing in mergers and acquisitions, and another with a small environmental services company. My client, a longtime environmentalist, was drawn to the smaller company, but it was clear the law firm could pay more and give her more business in the long run. Both projects required a detailed proposal; she didn't have time to do both, and had to choose.

Practicality dictated that she pursue the law firm project, but she kept feeling blocked. She procrastinated on writing the proposal, delayed following up, and didn't prepare well when she met with them. Ultimately, the law firm hired someone else.

She returned to the environmental services company, who luckily had not yet chosen a consultant for their project. Suddenly, writing the proposal became effortless, she was eager to follow up, and when she met with the company, her enthusiasm convinced them to hire her on the spot.

So, which one was the more lucrative choice?

In Mark Albion's book, *Making a Life, Making a Living,* he describes a study of 1,500 business school graduates that took place over twenty years. Based on their responses to a survey, the students were grouped into two categories.

Group A wanted to make money first, then pursue what they really wanted to do later when they had more resources. They comprised 83% of the respondents. Group B, who made up 17%, intended to pursue their true interests first, sure that money would eventually follow.

> Instead of considering first which direction is likely to be the most lucrative, start by determining which path will probably be the most fulfilling.

Twenty years later, there were a total of 101 millionaires in the two groups. Only one came from Group A. There were 100 millionaires out of the 255 people in Group B.

It appears that choosing happiness over money can be a valid business decision. There are some caveats, of course. You need to make sure that the course of action you are considering is a viable alternative, not an altruistic fantasy. My marketing consultant client had already determined that the environmental company had a budget to pay her. They just couldn't pay as much as the law firm, and it was a smaller project.

But her experience — and the business school study — suggest that a quite practical approach to decisions like these might be to begin this way. Instead of considering first which direction is likely to be the most lucrative, start by determining which path will probably be the most fulfilling. Then find a group of people, a type of project, or a line of work along that path that will pay you what you need to charge.

Our inner saboteurs are subtle. If one line of business or type of client makes you happier than another, you may find mysterious roadblocks appearing when you pursue business you really don't want. With no boss looking over your shoulder, you must find a compelling path, or your marketing will languish.

And when that happens, you won't get the business anyway.

FOUR STEPS
OUT OF MARKETING OVERWHELM

❖

Does it seem like there are just too many things to do in order to market your business? It's easy to get overwhelmed with marketing ideas, plans, and tasks, especially when many of them involve learning new skills. And people are always telling you about something else to do.

But you're only one person. You can only afford to pay for so much help. Is it really even possible to do everything about marketing that others say you should?

Here are four steps to find a clear path out of marketing overwhelm.

1. Decide what you're offering. One of the fastest ways to beat overwhelm is to narrow your focus to marketing only one product or service at a time. Yes, you may have a full menu of offerings, but you can't effectively market them all at once. The clearer you are about what you are marketing to whom, and when, the less overwhelmed you will be.

Every time you have to make a choice about what to do with your marketing, first choose what you will offer. For example, if you are a psychotherapist who offers individual therapy, group programs, and paid presentations, you might be trying to decide whether to market yourself with networking, building referral relationships, advertising, social media, or public speaking. Each one of those might be a good approach to use, depending on what you are offering.

Narrow your focus. Choose. For example, "This week I want to work on getting more clients for individual therapy." As soon as you make that declaration, you will have a frame of reference for making more decisions. Now you can ask yourself questions like, "How have I found most individual therapy clients in the past?" or "How do most of my colleagues find their individual therapy clients?" A likely route for you to take will start to emerge.

2. Get clear about your immediate goals. What do you need more of right now? What is coming up soon that you should prepare for? What problems do you need to address? Questions like these can help you determine what your primary objectives should be for marketing at this particular time.

Here's what a marketing goal might sound like:

- One new major client by the end of this month.
- Three new ongoing clients by December 31st.
- Take advantage of next week's speaking engagement to sign up at least two new clients for my service.
- Increase the number of website visitors who opt in to my mailing list by 25%.

> Don't be distracted by "opportunities" that find their way into your email, voice mail, or social media stream... This week, and today, do only what you already said you'd do.

Including a quantity and timeframe in your goal will help you determine the best way to accomplish it. For example, if you want one new major client by the end of the month, it's unlikely you will achieve that by attending networking events or increasing your social media activity. You will more likely need to focus on following up with prospects you already have, and further developing existing relationships.

3. Choose just a few specific things to do. When you have a long list of varied tasks to accomplish, it's difficult not to feel overwhelmed by it. This is especially true when some of the items are stated in a vague or general way. Consider what you plan to offer and what your immediate goal is. What are a few activities that are most likely to take you in that direction? Get as specific as possible. For example:

- Contact three new possible referral sources for individual clients this week and invite them to coffee sometime this month.
- Place follow-up phone calls to five prospective clients per day for my monthly retainer service, and send an email when I don't reach them.
- Spend thirty minutes each day interacting on social media with people who are likely candidates for my new program.
- Write a twenty-page ebook that will appeal to clients for my assessment package, to use as a bonus gift for opting in to my mailing list.

Resist any temptation to record every activity you can think of. List what seems like about a week's worth of items, then stop. Revisit your list next week to revise or add to it. If you think of items you'd like to address sometime, but which don't make sense to tackle this week, put them on a "Maybe" list that you can refer to weekly when you revise your current list. Don't keep looking at ideas or tasks you aren't currently working on; that is a sure road to overwhelm.

4. Do only what you said. Give yourself permission to have the activities you put on this week's list be the only things you do about marketing. This can be one of the most difficult challenges of avoiding marketing overwhelm, but it's essential. Don't be distracted by "opportunities" that find their way into your email, voice mail, or social media stream. If they seem potentially helpful, put them on your Maybe list, and consider them next week. This week, and today, do only what you already said you'd do.

Marketing does not need to be overwhelming. All you need is a simple, targeted plan. Follow these four steps, and you'll soon find yourself producing greatly improved results with much less effort.

MARKETING WITH THE 80/20 RULE

❖

You know about the 80/20 rule, right? It's the guideline that 80% of your return comes from 20% of your investment. For example, 80% of your referrals come from 20% of the people in your network. 80% of your new business comes from 20% of your prospects. 80% of your new contacts come from 20% of your networking activities. And so on.

Like all such guidelines, this one is inexact, but helpful. If used correctly, it makes you stop and think. Where are most of your results coming from? And where is most of your effort going? Imagine how much less time and money you could spend on marketing if you could simply identify the 20% of your current efforts that are really the only ones that matter. You could let go of 80% of what you're doing.

I can't guarantee everyone can do this. Some of you are already pretty smart about how you market yourselves. But here are some places to look.

1. Where are your clients actually coming from? You may think you know the answer to this question, but I find in many cases that people's assumptions don't match the data. Review every client you've worked with in the past two years and try to determine how that client entered your life. Make a list of not just the source of each client, but what you may have done (or made available) to produce clients from that source.

For example, "Referred by Mary Smith. Met her for coffee last month," or "Inquiry from my website. Signed up for my special report two weeks ago." If you can't uncover data like this about every new client, now is the time to start tracking it for the future.

Notice any patterns this analysis suggests, and strategize how you might reproduce these successes. Where could you find more referral sources like Mary Smith? Or what potential referral sources already in your network have you yet to meet for coffee? If most of the new clients originating from your website are those that requested your special report, is that request form available on every page?

2. Where are your highest paying or lowest hassle clients coming from? The quality of your clients can make as much difference to the success of your business as the quantity of them. Select the top 20% of your clients from the list you made above — either the ones that paid you the most or troubled you the least — and consider how you might acquire more clients like them.

> When you can see exactly where your clients are coming from, you can also determine where you're paying too much to get them.

Notice not just the source of these top clients, but also what characteristics they might share. You might discover that your highest paying clients are those who themselves are in a higher income bracket. Or that the clients who give you the least trouble are the ones who have worked with professionals in your line of business before. These are valuable clues to where the majority of your marketing efforts should go.

3. What marketing approaches are costing you more money than they bring in? When you can see exactly where your clients are coming from, you can also determine where you're paying too much to get them. Common places for overspending are online and print directory listings, pay-per-click ads, search engine optimization fees, and multiple association memberships.

Compare not just what you are spending on each potential source of clients to what revenue you received from it, but what profit you ultimately made. A $500 ad that brought you one $500 client has earned you nothing. And an ad that produces many inquiries but little paying business consumes time you could better use to produce income.

4. What are you currently doing that you haven't gotten a single client from? Some marketing techniques take time to pay off, but if you've been using a particular approach for several months and no clients have yet resulted, it's time to reconsider. You probably need to either abandon this approach or fine-tune it.

If you belong to a networking group that isn't producing referrals for you, consider whether you should seek a different group that's a better match for your target market, or stick with the group and start meeting its members individually for coffee. If you've been cold calling corporate prospects without results, you may need to drop cold calling and focus on referrals and introductions.

By making judicious use of the 80/20 rule, you can eliminate the least productive marketing activities you engage in and ramp up those that are more effective. You can also focus most of your marketing on the sources for clients and type of prospects that have worked well for you in the past. And that can put you in the 20% of entrepreneurs who have a successful business instead of in the 80% who don't.

IF YOU CAN'T MAKE A LIVING, HOW CAN YOU MAKE A DIFFERENCE?

❖

What made you decide to go into business for yourself? Did you want to make more money, gain more freedom, enjoy yourself more, or make more of an impact on the world? For many self-employed professionals, the desire to help others as well as themselves plays a significant role in their decision. Helping people may even have been your primary motivation for choosing the type of work you do.

However, not all of us who set out to help others through our businesses succeed at it. In fact, many of the best-intentioned professionals fail at building a sustainable business or private practice. It seems that the skills and mindset of helping others don't always match those needed to build a profitable business.

If you're in business because you want to make a difference, help others, and contribute your unique gifts, you may be handicapped in marketing and sales because so much of your focus is on other people's desires and needs. You may feel that asking someone to buy from you is an imposition, that talking about yourself doesn't serve others, or that self-promotion is somehow inappropriate if your primary aim is to help people.

But here's the reality. If you can't make a living doing what you do, you won't be able to make a difference. If people don't hire you, you don't get to share your gifts. If no one knows your business exists, you won't have the opportunity to help people. If your business fails, you'll have to go back to making a living some other way, and never get a chance to make the impact you know that you could.

So long as you're stuck in the struggle of not quite making a living, not only are you not making an impact with your business, you are held back from making one in other ways too. You don't have enough time available to volunteer for causes you believe in. You don't have the money to support those causes with donations. You may not even be able to adequately support those most important to you — your family.

When you look at the disparity between your present situation and your goals in that light, you may begin to see that perhaps sales and marketing is not such a selfish endeavor. When the purpose of your business is to help people, letting more people know what you do contributes to much more than your own pocketbook.

In the standard airline safety briefing, they advise that in case of emergency, you should put on your own oxygen mask first. What would happen if you began to look at marketing this way? To be in a position to serve other people, you must be able to sustain yourself. When your own survival is guaranteed, you'll have the strength, resources, and peace of mind to assist others.

> To be in a position to serve other people, you must be able to sustain yourself. When your own survival is guaranteed, you'll have the strength, resources, and peace of mind to assist others.

The next time you find yourself fearful, resistant, or immobilized about marketing, remember that you are not in business for yourself alone. Picture in your mind's eye the people you most want to serve. Visualize how you can make a difference in the world by helping more people.

Determine that your business will not only survive, but thrive, so that your gifts will be allowed their fullest expression. In order to truly help others, you may first need to help yourself.

ABOUT THE AUTHOR

C.J. Hayden is a San Francisco business coach, and the author of five other books, including the bestselling *Get Clients Now!* Since 1992, she's been helping self-employed professionals land more clients with less effort.

The *Get Clients Now!* book is now in its third edition, and has been translated into multiple languages. Thousands of consultants, coaches, and professionals around the world have made *Get Clients Now!* their marketing bible.

The pieces selected for this book originally appeared in a wide variety of publications, including *Bay Area Business Woman, Enterprising Women, Professional Services Advisor, Rainmaker Report, Small Business Coach,* C.J.'s blog, and the *Get Clients Now! E-Letter.*

A popular speaker and workshop leader, C.J. has presented hundreds of programs on marketing, entrepreneurship, and overcoming barriers to success, for international audiences. She has taught marketing for John F. Kennedy University, Mills College, the U.S. Small Business Administration, and SCORE.

C.J. holds the credentials Master Certified Coach from the International Coach Federation, and Certified Professional Co-Active Coach from the Coaches Training Institute. She has completed advanced coach training with the Arbinger Institute.

To find out more about C.J.'s books, home-study courses, or how to work with her personally, visit www.getclientsnow.com.

Made in the USA
Coppell, TX
18 February 2020